Walk Santa Barbara

Cheri Rae &
John McKinney

Walk
Santa Barbara
CITY · COAST · COUNTRY

OLYMPUS PRESS

SANTA BARBARA

For Daniel and Sophia
May Santa Barbara always be at your feet.

Book design and typography by Jim Cook
Map design and cartography by Hélène Webb
Cover photography by Siewshien Sam, Elliot Sam Photography
Principal photography by Djamel E. Ramoul

ACKNOWLEDGMENTS
For their unflagging encouragement, we thank our friends and family, fellow Sierra Clubbers, and our writing and publishing colleagues, including Fran Rosenberg, Diane and John Bock, Michael Moore, Susan Petty, Bob McDermott and Marcia Meier. A special thanks goes to Guy Walker and The Wayfarers, and to the wayfarers from all across the country who've spent their holidays walking in Santa Barbara and giving us great feedback.

For sharing the city's rich history, thanks to the Santa Barbara Historical Society, Pearl Chase Society, and neighbors in the Historic Bungalow District. We appreciate the help of Santa Barbara's lively hospitality community including Susan Lehman and the Four Seasons Biltmore, Janis Claphoff and the San Ysidro Ranch. A special thanks goes to the many businesses and community members that support the Take a Vacation From Your Car and Car-Free Santa Barbara programs initiated by the Santa Barbara County Air Pollution Control District.

For assisting us with our wine country walks, we raise our glasses in thanks to the Santa Ynez Valley Women Hikers, Fran Murray of Murray Vineyards, and the friendly staff of Firestone Vineyards.

For assistance with walks on the wild side of Santa Barbara, we extend our thanks to the many rangers and administrators of the Channel Coast District of the California Department of Parks and Recreation, the National Park Service (Channel Islands National Park and the Gaviota Coast Project), the Land Trust of Santa Barbara County, Los Padres National Forest, The Dunes Center, Sedgwick Reserve, Santa Barbara County Parks Department and retired Parks director Mike Pahos, Naturalist Liz Mason and her staff at Cachuma Lake County Park.

Stand Fast, Santa Barbara!

Romance is the greatest asset of California. It has been for more than 350 years. To all this centuried romance, Santa Barbara is legitimate and favorite heiress—about the only one left that has not yet traded away her birthright.

You hold that last of California which has shone for centuries in song and story, which has fascinated the world and put a new sentiment and beauty in American life.

—CHARLES F. LUMMIS
Santa Barbara Morning Press, 1923

Table of Contents

Coast / 89

Country / 155

Reference

What's Afoot
in Santa Barbara

SANTA BARBARA isn't any bigger than the seventy or so suburbs surrounding L.A., but it's a world apart, the Southern California of old postcards not present-day headlines.

It (well, its architectural style, anyway) all started with the great quake of 1925 that destroyed much of downtown. After the quake, city mothers and fathers realized they had a great opportunity to create a unique-looking community.

We can marvel at not only how well Santa Barbara was rebuilt from ruins, but how quickly; scarcely a year after its disaster, the Better Homes in America jury judged Santa Barbara to be the most beautiful residential community in the nation.

Some long-time residents think it still is.

We think beauty is very much in the eyes of the beholder, and believe a better boast might be that Santa Barbara is one of the nation's most walk-able cities. In fact, Santa Barbara is more pedestrian-friendly than most Euro-towns and lacks only international signage and some imaginative civic promotion to become one of the world's great walking destinations.

Walk through Santa Barbara and admire the magnificent natural setting and beautiful architecture, hear the birds and church bells, fill your lungs with the tangy salt air, feel the sunshine on your shoulders. Read the unique commemorative tiles that mark historical events, stop at a sidewalk café for lunch or a lattè, browse the bookstores, or wind through the paseos.

We figure one walk is all most visitors need to realize what Santa Barbara is not: a place where everyone is rich; a locale that resembles the glitzy Santa Barbara of the once long-running TV soap opera; a town once demographically scorned as the home of the newly-wed and nearly dead; a distant suburb of LA. One walk is all visitors need to see the town for what it is: a modern city that's proud of its history; a small town that offers big-city services; a seaside resort that attracts visitors from across the nation and around the world.

Walking is by no means the only way to see Santa Barbara. Rent a car,

The breakwater is a working harbor, a place for pleasure craft, and a wonderful destination for a stroll.

as thousands do, use that that terrible tourist map you downloaded from some weird site like www.weknoweverythingabouttravelingevery where.com and get lost like everyone else. (We Santa Barbarans are always happy to give directions, explain where you missed the turn for the Mission, and try to talk you out of eating at certain tourist traps.)

No, walking isn't the only way to see Santa Barbara; it's simply the best way. Other cities in the world have a beautiful city center, an inspiring coastline, a wine country and a rugged backcountry, but only Santa Barbara has all four and is so inviting to walkers.

Hardly a month goes by without some L.A.-based celebs reporting how much they enjoyed a weekend hike in Santa Barbara. We've spotted some on the trail and lots in town.

True Santa Barbarans consider it very uncool to approach a celebrity; in fact, the more blasé you can act in a celeb's presence and the more you ignore the visiting or resident media darling, the better. Add a little pretend anonymity to the enjoyment of Santa Barbara's good restaurants and even better mountain trails and you start to understand why celebs—and lesser-known folks—hike here.

Walk Santa Barbara's main street (State Street) a mile to the beach. Get a boost along the way at what is likely the greatest concentration of cappuccino parlors south of Seattle. (How can Santa Barbarans drink so much coffee and remain so mellow?) If a double espresso doesn't revive you, take the electric shuttle bus (25 cents) from the beach back up State Street.

By day State Street is filled with a dozen languages as visitors shop the day away in the pleasant paseos while laptop-toting locals (very hard-working; the cost of paradise is dear) scurry from meeting to meeting. The character of State Street completely changes after dark: diners and filmgoers replace shoppers on the sidewalk: theaters turn on their neon signs, restaurants and nightclubs open their doors, and everybody checks out everybody else.

Walk a block east on Anapamu to the famed Santa Barbara County Courthouse, a huge, gleaming white, Spanish Colonial Revival building that is one of the most distinctive public structures in America. The Mediterranean-to-the-max edifice seems a Hollywood stage set to some, more than a bit over the top.

Sure we locals sometimes tire of the city's Spanish architecture and all that white-washed stucco and black iron grillwork around town seems a little too precious. Sometimes we identify with private eye Kinsey Millhone, created by Santa Barbara mystery novelist Sue Grafton, who just knows there must be no good behind those sun-bedazzled walls and jaundiced palms, that there just has to be something rotten in paradise.

But most of the time we admire Santa Barbara's architectural consistency (even the McDonald's is done in Mission motif), the town's tenacious resistance to change, and its ability to combine a Southern California lifestyle with a Northern California sensibility. Evidence of this south-north combination is displayed in the newsracks around town, where both the *Los Angeles Times* and *San Francisco Chronicle* are widely available.

Best view of the micropolis is from atop the courthouse clock-tower, where you get oriented for your next walk. With the help of the huge compass painted on the roof, notice the east-west trend of the coastline and the mountains. The south-facing Santa Barbara coast and the Santa Ynez Mountains behind the city gather a soft, magical Mediterranean light that's very special.

Tour Mission Santa Barbara, stroll the nearby rose garden, then walk up to the oh-so-close-but-missed-by-many Museum of Natural History and adjacent perfect-for-a-picnic Rocky Nook Park.

Off-the-tourist-track trails abound at the Santa Barbara Botanic Garden, a sprawling homage to California's native flora. Downtown, at Micheltorena and Garden Streets, is another botanical delight, Alice Keck Park Memorial Garden, a shady sanctuary surrounding a lily pond. Kids like watching the carp swim and turtles bask and love the playground at the park across the street—a wooden extravaganza of swings, slides, pirate ship, castle and anyone's guess—called Kid's World guaranteed to exhaust even the most energetic of children

A walk way off the beaten path is an ocean bluff stroll through the Santa Barbara Cemetery, located at the east end of Cabrillo Boulevard near the Highway 101 off-ramp. Begin at the graceful Romanesque-Gothic chapel, long regarded as one of the masterpieces of premier Santa Barbara architect George Washington Smith. Inside, view the stunning frescoes of famed Mexican painter Alfredo Ramos Martinez. Next, walk the grounds, glimpsing the tombstones of Santa Barbara's rich and famous and enjoying the lovely view of the harbor. Notice that even after death the wealthiest citizens have the best coastal property with stunning views.

At sunset, walk the waterfront near Stearns Wharf with fellow visitors from around the world. Better yet, walk atop the breakwater around the harbor or promenade nearby Shoreline Park with the locals.

Take a beach walk. Leave behind the tourist-jammed strand near Stearns Wharf and join the locals two miles upcoast on Hendry's Beach at Arroyo Burro County Park. Parking is free and the uncrowded beach extends six miles to the University of California Santa Barbara. Do watch your step though; Santa Barbara dogs do what dogs everywhere do on the beach, as do horses (yes, horses) ridden down to the beach by the horsey-set luxury homeowners of Hope Ranch from the bluffs above.

Don't miss a stroll through one of Santa Barbara's foothill canyons—Rattlesnake and Cold Spring are the locals' favorites. Smell the sage, listen to the murmur of a little creek, experience the thousand and one pleasures of the trail.

❧

This book is your invitation to explore a place like no other, an opportunity to walk through neighborhoods that beckon, through a natural world that delights. Walking Santa Barbara is a chance for visitors to get an intimate look, for busy natives a chance to slow down and smell the roses.

We've offered more than sixty of our favorite walks, short and long, nearby and far away, for your enjoyment. Even the most casual stroller will find Santa Barbara a pedestrian-friendly town and be able to navigate to the major sights with this guide. The practiced walker and avid hiker will also find in these pages many miles of pathways to follow.

A word about walking. Now that we've preached the gospel of walking, we hope you won't lose confidence in the authors if we confess just a little ambivalence about the word. The popular media image of a walker these days is one of those overheated, arm-swinging, watch-

watching fitness freaks. No, the walker we have in mind is at least as interested in aesthetics as athletics.

Other words have their merit. Certainly strolling is a way to go. Sauntering conveys a certain *joie de vivre*. Even hiking is okay; this guide includes backcountry trails that will challenge the avid hiker.

Actually, the word we like best for the spirit we wish to convey is Spanish and has no English counterpart. The word is *paseo*. A paseo can be loosely translated as a leisurely walk, an un-businesslike excursion, a pleasurable picnic. A paseo is also a special place; you'll visit many of them in Santa Barbara.

There's a pathway—through the city, the coast, the country—waiting to take you wherever you want to go.

The Spanish named not only the journey but the destinations; today, Spanish street names abound. The early Catholic padres also named peaks, valleys, rivers and canyons after their favorite saints, and Spanish words make up much of our geographical vocabulary: *cañon, rio, arroyo, punta, camino, mar.*

But Santa Barbara has embraced not only the culture of its first Spanish, and later Mexican, inhabitants, it has borrowed liberally from the entire Mediterranean. And the city has used its Mediterranean style to sell itself to the world—"See America's Riviera" invited the travel brochures. Declared an 1886 brochure: "Travelers in quest of the beautiful may no longer 'See Naples and die'; but visit Santa Barbara and live."

Santa Barbara is a Mediterranean city nestled in a picturesque setting that easily rivals any Old World locale. The word "Mediterranean" conjures up images of white buildings with tiled roofs and wrought-iron gates; stone-lined walkways and colorful plazas; alfresco dining in a convivial atmosphere; warm breezes and palm-lined beaches. It also suggests a civilized style, an appreciation for arts and culture, casual living, and warm, inviting hospitality.

But Santa Barbara is more than a Mediterranean city. It's a Mediterranean coast as well. In Santa Barbara, waves lap at broad, sandy beaches; a fleet of fishing boats bob in the harbor and palm trees sway in the cooling breeze. And walkers stroll along the sand, glimpsing dolphins as they surface, and marvel at the rugged beauty of the nearby Channel Islands.

Getting to know Santa Barbara means walking on the coast, in the city, and in the country as well. In the city, lovely residential neighborhoods suggest leisurely strolling; shaded paseos offer unique shopping, and a few frankly tourist-y destinations simply should not be missed. But if you never stray from the sidewalk, and head into the backcountry far from the shops and parking lots, you won't really see Santa Barbara. A variety of trails head straight into the natural beauty and colorful history of the local mountains.

Santa Barbara Yesterday and Today

ON JUNE 29, 1925, a severe earthquake shook Santa Barbara, damaging and destroying much of downtown. While human casualties were fortunately few, the damage to buildings was severe. After the quake, citizens and civic leaders realized it was a chance for Santa Barbara, as one architect put it, "to make of itself the most romantic, beautiful and best-planned city in Western America."

What followed, particularly during the years 1925–30 was the full flowering of Mission Revival and Spanish Revival architecture that today makes Santa Barbara so distinctive. How that particular look was adopted, and along with it a Mediterranean lifestyle, is a story that begins more than a century-and-a-half before the big earthquake.

It's a story of the Chumash, Spanish, Mexican and American and European peoples. Each group was influenced by succeeding powers; present-day Santa Barbara owes much of its richness to its past.

The first people to inhabit the Santa Barbara area were the Chumash. For nearly 10,000 years, the population flourished in the mild climate, subsisting on the abundant food sources they found in the waters and on the land. They were excellent fishermen who navigated the waters of the Channel Islands in plank canoes known as *tomolo*. Although their society was preliterate, their basketry and rock drawings indicate a sophisticated knowledge of astronomy, and other artifacts suggest the Chumash were accomplished traders and architects, as well as a people of deep spiritual commitment.

The arrival of the Spanish signaled the decline, and eventual end, of Santa Barbara's native population. In 1542, Portuguese navigator Juan Rodríguez Cabrillo, sailing for Spain, was the first European to glimpse the Santa Barbara coast. Some years later, in 1602, a priest who served the crew of Sebastian Vizcaino named the area in honor of Saint Barbara.

Sergeant José Francisco de Ortega, who served as a trail scout to California explorer Captain Gaspar de Portolá, was the first European to set foot in the area, in 1769. Some years later, Ortega was appointed to be the first commandante of the Santa Barbara royal fortress, a military outpost established to defend and maintain the Spanish empire's claim

Saint Barbara

WHEN EXPLORER Sebastian Vizcaino's crewmen found their tiny ship tossed about by a nasty storm on the eve of St. Barbara's Day in 1602, they prayed for her to intervene and save them from a cruel death at sea. When the day dawned, and the ship found safe harbor, the grateful men named this coastal refuge for the saint.

Saint Barbara, whose father beheaded her after she embraced Christianity in defiance of his beliefs, symbolizes courage, faith and virtue to Christians all over the world.

Mission Santa Barbara was consecrated on its present site on December 4, 1786, coinciding with the feast day of the martyred Saint Barbara. Saint Barbara Greek Orthodox Church, located in the Santa Barbara foothills on San Antonio Road, holds a special service and celebration on the saint's name day.

to the area. The Mission was founded to reinforce the Spanish empire's religious interest as well.

Santa Barbara was affected by international relations when Mexico revolted against Spanish rule; the Treaty of Córdova transferred Spain's California holdings to Mexico in 1822.

During the short period of Mexican rule, the Mission was secularized, and much of its property was divided into ranchos, where many residents participated in the hide-and-tallow trade. Former soldiers married local women, built adobe-tile-roofed houses and settled into comfortable lives.

The streets of Santa Barbara bear the names of many of the influential families of this time: de la Guerra, Carrillo, Cota and Gutierrez among them. Social festivities were colorful and frequent; in the classic, *Two Years Before the Mast,* Richard Henry Dana described a three-day wedding celebration.

Most of western North American came under American control with the conclusion of the Mexican-American War in 1848. In quick succession, Santa Barbara was designated a county seat, incorporated as a city, and became part of the state of California, which entered the Union on September 9, 1850.

The city was surveyed in 1851 by a sea captain who possessed ques-

Viva la Fiesta! Celebrate the romance of Santa Barbara's early days each August.

tionable credentials; his unfortunately sloppy work resulted in a city grid that runs curiously counter to the norm. Santa Barbara's northeast-northwest (rather than north-south) orientation has confused visitors and residents ever since.

In his 1873 travel guide, *California: For Health, Pleasure, and Residence,* Charles Nordhoff extolled the virtues of Santa Barbara's mild climate, scenic location, and abundant natural hot springs in the nearby backcountry. His enthusiasm surely helped establish Santa Barbara as a desirable destination for "invalids," as they called them in Victorian times.

But before the city's reputation as "the Sanitarium of the Pacific" got too firmly entrenched, boosters began building luxury residences and accommodations and marketing Santa Barbara as an upscale winter resort town for the East Coast and European wealthy. As transportation to Santa Barbara improved (the completion of Stearns Wharf passenger steamer dock, the completion of the Southern Pacific tracks and train depot), a more middle-class visitor came to holiday.

Pearl Chase

During the first two decades of the twentieth century, two industries took hold in Santa Barbara. One was the airplane factory run by the Lockheed brothers, the other was the Flying A Film Studios, which at one time had the largest and most modern production facility in the world. Alas, for Santa Barbara's future as an aerospace center and/or entertainment capital, Lockheed moved south to Burbank, the Flying A to Hollywood.

After the city's miraculous and creative recovery from the devastating earthquake of 1925, the town gained an even more enhanced reputation as a playground to the rich and famous. Max Fleischmann, the yeast magnate, and actors such as Rita Hayworth, and Charlie Chaplin enjoyed their Santa Barbara retreats.

John F. Kennedy and his bride, Jacqueline, honeymooned at the San Ysidro Ranch in Montecito in 1953. During Ronald Reagan's presidency, from 1981 to 1989, Santa Barbara was known as the "Western White House" and was deluged by reporters and politicians whenever the president made one of his frequent visits to his hilltop ranch.

While politicians and movie stars (many entertainers make their homes in Santa Barbara today) gained Santa Barbara nationwide publicity, some prominent locals worked behind the scenes to make the city a very special place.

Thomas Storke founded the city's daily newspaper, the *Santa Barbara News-Press* in 1901 and ran it until 1964, when he retired at the age of 88. Storke successfully pushed for the major projects that have defined the region: the creation of Lake Cachuma that give the city a dependable water supply; establishing the harbor and airport; bringing a University of California campus to Santa Barbara, and much more.

Working behind the scenes to give the city its aesthetic sense was Pearl Chase who, for a half century, chaired the city's Plans and Planting Committee. After graduating from college in 1909 she returned to Santa Barbara and began a seventy-year crusade to beautify and preserve the city. Under her influence, the city established strict architectural, zoning and environmental guidelines. She founded the Trust for Historic Preservation, the annual Old Spanish Days Fiesta, the Council of Christmas Cheer and many more civic institutions.

The 1969 Santa Barbara oil spill put Santa Barbara on the national map in a less flattering way, but even in this tragic instance, the local citizenry managed to put its best foot forward. The "environmental shot hear 'round the world" galvanized local conservationists and most of the community has taken a strong environmental stance ever since. Employment in Santa Barbara has traditionally been in the defense and high-tech research fields, along with a heavy emphasis on tourism and retail sales. Santa Barbara is home to several successful catalog companies, a large number of book publishers, and the greatest concentration of restaurateurs this side of San Francisco.

Beginning in the 1980s, the Santa Barbara wine industry emerged from near obscurity to national, and now international prominence. The Santa Ynez Valley Wine Country produces world-class wines and offers the traveler a beautiful place to taste and tour.

The community has a thriving high-tech sector nicknamed Silicon Beach and a number of scientific research companies. Commercial space launches from Vandenberg Air Force Base are 21st-century business opportunities that excite many Santa Barbarans.

❦

For its size (just 18 square miles, population less than 100,000), Santa Barbara offers a surprising number of cultural attractions: first-class theaters, museums of art and natural history, a symphony orchestra, several colleges and a university, and many regularly scheduled festivals celebrating the city's unique historic and ethnic heritages.

There's certainly been trouble in paradise. The city has survived its share of natural disasters, including several earthquakes and devastating fires (the Painted Cave Fire of 1990 that received international attention). Periods of extended drought have plagued the area; residents and visitors must carefully conserve precious water resources. And, as in most American cities, the political debates continue to rage over issues that include growth/no-growth, economic issues, the stratospheric cost of housing, quality of the local schools, historic preservation vs. development, plus questions about how best to help the poor and unfortunate.

Still, Santa Barbara remains one of the most desirable destinations in the world. What visitors—especially those who walk Santa Barbara—discover is a modern city that's proud of its history, a small town that offers big-city services, a caring community where neighbors still know each other and extend themselves to those in need.

City

STAND AT the edge of historic Stearns Wharf, under the seven flags of California, and for a moment contemplate this land as it was first viewed from the sea by explorers far from home. It was a pretty place then, this small crescent of land nestled between shoreline and rugged peaks, and it remains lovely today. About the time the American Revolution raged on the other side of this great continent, they established a military outpost and a religious one—on sites that can be visited today.

From this simple history, a complex heritage has grown, a city has been built and matured, a civilization has flowered, a mythology has been told. This lovely land has become home to generations, playground for rich and famous, destination for latter-day explorers seeking their own glimpse of paradise on the Pacific.

In Santa Barbara, memorable images overlap and merge, like snapshots in an old scrapbook recently revised. Here one American president-to-be (John F. Kennedy) honeymooned with his lovely bride, another played volleyball on the beach (Bill Clinton) and yet another famously cleared brush on his nearby ranch (Ronald Reagan), often called the Western White House. It's a place where not only politicians, but movie stars, rock idols and television characters shed their larger-than life personae, and disappear into luxurious mansions, only to be seen quietly dining at local trattorias, donating to worthy causes, and patronizing the local arts scene. It's a place where world-renowned writers, photographers and artists seek refuge and find inspiration to continue their work. It's a place of fandangos and fiestas, where the cultures of the world are celebrated no less than the wonders of nature.

Yet Santa Barbara is so much more than a stop on the jet-setter's tour of fine and memorable places. It's where families come to enjoy the beaches, the playgrounds and the parks, where couples come for a romantic getaway, where seniors come for a quiet retreat. It's a place where both long-time residents and the newly arrived strive to maintain the quality of life that attracted them to settle in Santa Barbara.

Residents know the distinct charms of the neighborhoods, where stately Victorians stand side-by-side with California cottages and Craftsman bungalows. They squire more than their share of out-of-town guests about town with a casual nonchalance about the beauty that surrounds them. Those who live here attend lectures and performances, dine at a stunning array of restaurants and walk along the shore, knowing all the while that the amenities offered here are greater than those offered in most cities many times the size of Santa Barbara. Exemplifying the grace and generosity that have long characterized this small town that's grown way up, locals are happy to share, delighted that so many visitors find so much pleasure in the place they call home.

The lovely buildings and lush greenery as viewed from the wharf hide a wealth of latter-day riches only imagined by fortune seekers who came to these shores so many years ago. Take a walk and see for yourself. You'll discover that the pleasures of the city are innumerable and unexpected—a flower-filled courtyard off a hidden paseo, a bubbling fountain, an artfully simple historic adobe, a tile mural commemorating a visit by the Queen of England, a shopping district that retains a quiet charm. It's a place where quiet quality wins out over conspicuous consumption—at least most of the time.

All that's best about Santa Barbara requires—demands—discovery on foot. It's where you really can slow down and savor the beauty in the details of a very special city.

Mission Santa Barbara Museum of Natural History

Less than a mile, but a long time on your feet

The Santa Barbara Mission is on every visitor's itinerary, and for good reason. The "Queen of the Missions," along with its exhibit hall, grounds and gardens, provides insights into California's earliest beginnings.

Don't miss the Mission's neighbor, the Santa Barbara Museum of Natural History, which offers an exploration of the human and natural history of Santa Barbara. Dioramas and displays orient the visitor to the natural environment—botanical, geological, oceanic and more—and offer a hint of what the walker can experience by roaming the Santa Barbara coast and backcountry—less than a mile, but a long time on your feet.

Pack a lunch and plan a picnic at lovely Rocky Nook Park, located just a block from the museum. The oak-shaded park is studded with massive Mission Creek boulders; it's a great place for adults to relax, kids to play.

Mission Santa Barbara is open 9 A.M. to 5 P.M. daily; 1-5 P.M. on Sundays; admission fee. Santa Barbara Museum of Natural History is open 9 A.M. to 5 P.M. Monday through Saturday; 10 A.M. to 5 P.M. on Sunday; admission fee.

Directions: Exit Highway 101 on Mission Street and head east to Laguna Street. Turn left and drive a few blocks to the Mission.

MTD: Line 22 Old Mission to the Santa Barbara Mission.

The Walk: Take in the Mission's self-guided tour, which begins in the gift shop. You'll examine historic photos, interpretive proclamations, and a re-creation of a Franciscan padre's bedroom and the Mission kitchen.

You'll visit the Mission sanctuary, still in use today, as is the small chapel. Pause in the Sacred Garden to admire the succulents (the garden was closed to women visitors, except political wives and royalty, until 1959). Don't miss viewing the beautiful bell tower, which chimes each morning at six o'clock.

Cross the threshold, marked by a skull-and-crossbones, into the historic Mission cemetery. Among the vaults, plots and mausoleums are the remains of some 4,000 Indians and many prominent Santa Barbara families. Those familiar with the children's classic, *Island of the Blue Dolphins*, will notice a significant plaque on the wall. It marks the final

The great California condors passed this way, and may do so once again.

resting place of the young woman, Juana Maria, known as "The Lost Woman of San Nicholas," whose story was fictionalized in the book.

Exiting the cemetery and ending the Mission tour, look for twin sycamore trees standing nearby. As the legend goes, the trees were planted by sympathetic Mission Father O'Keefe to protect the Indian women from the sun as they took water from the aqueduct. Admire the view from the Mission steps, and scout the adjacent asphalt parking lot for faded artwork. Every Memorial Day weekend, the parking lot becomes a kaleidoscope of color as artists interpret the Old Masters and create one-of-a-kind artwork at the "I Madonnari" Street Painting Festival.

Enjoy the whimsical sculpted bear heads of the lavendaria, where Chumash women once laundered clothing. Over the years, the stone carvings on the bubbling Moorish fountain have been worn down by water and lime deposits.

Cross upper Laguna Street and head downhill over the wide lawn of the Mission to the rose garden located in Mission Historical Park. Species from all over the world are lovingly tended by volunteers; don't miss the picture-perfect view of the Mission framed by roses.

Following the sidewalk on the right (west side) of Laguna, then carefully crossing Alameda Padre Serra, take a look at the remains of stone structures built by the padres and the Chumash. The aqueduct, a grist mill, pottery house and two reservoirs have survived several earthquakes and the ravages of time, and still stand among the pepper trees and palms.

Walk up Mission Canyon Road above the Mission to Rocky Nook Park. You'll pass a watering trough at the corner of Mountain Drive, placed here in memory of a former resident "who loved this cañon." Cross a handsome stone bridge over Mission Creek, and explore boulder-strewn and oak-studded Rocky Nook Park. It's an excellent picnic spot, and a good place to relax before taking in the Museum of Natural History.

Don't miss the whimsical mosaics of two not-too-ferocious-looking reptiles lounging on the rocks lining Mission Creek. They are creations of local artist Dan Chrynko, whose work can be seen in many spots in town.

"I can see that this museum has been built by the work of love," said Albert Einstein when he visited the Santa Barbara Museum of Natural History in 1931. It's an evaluation that pretty well sums up the efforts of uncounted volunteers, researchers and benefactors who have made the museum such a special place.

The marine exhibit alone is worth the trip; it's so complete one young visitor recently asked, "But where's the mermaid?" With stunning displays of a Robust Hooked Squid, a brilliant mural of the food web, and a fascinating wave machine, you'll learn plenty about Santa Barbara's offshore environment.

Bugs and birds, mammals and reptiles, rocks and flowers—all are displayed here with an emphasis on what can be found nearby.

Cultural exhibits provide an excellent perspective on the human occupation of this land. You'll view artifacts created by the Chumash people who once populated coastal Santa Barbara. Basketry and rock art, musical instruments and games, clothing and trading beads provide a glimpse of long-ago days.

The wooded museum grounds contain science classrooms, an education center, a planetarium, and a handsome stone amphitheater. Field trips, lectures, workshops and volunteer programs are regularly sponsored by the museum. The museum gift shop stocks a selection of books and souvenir items.

If you're using the bus, catch it at the stop right out in front of the museum.

A history of Mission Santa Barbara

THE FIRST MISSION building was a rustic structure assembled of branches; it was replaced first with an adobe structure with a thatched roof, and that was replaced by a tile-topped adobe building hat was destroyed in a massive earthquake in 1812.

The stone edifice that stands today was begun in 1815, and was completed five years later. The earthquake of 1925 damaged the structure, but extensive and lengthy rebuilding efforts have successfully kept the "Queen of the Missions" in a remarkable state of repair. Few of California's missions have been so well-preserved.

Padre Antonio Ripoll designed the Mission, based on the designs of Vitruvius, a Roman architect who lived in the first century B.C., in the time of Caesar Augustus. Fr. Ripoll added a pair of Ionic columns along with the twin-domed towers. The striking building is notable for its majestic dominance of the surrounding area. Gazing at it today, one can only imagine how it might have looked a century ago, when only fields, orchards and a dirt path shared the scene.

Always more than just a church building, the Mission represents the efforts of the Church to convert the native population to Christianity. This issue of the missionaries' treatment of the Indians is a somewhat ticklish subject even today.

The Franciscan padres were no doubt convinced they were saving pagan Indians from an eternity of damnation, and determined to change the customs and religious beliefs of the hunter-gatherers they encountered in the New World. The two cultures obviously clashed.

Unwilling or unable to surrender their traditional ways and beliefs, many Chumash died of stress and from exposure to European diseases. Besides relocating and changing their ways, the natives were also expected to provide the Missionary fathers with a free—if not always willing—source of labor. In addition to building the Mission itself, the Chumash helped construct the extensive aqueduct system and reservoirs that provided Santa Barbara with water. Forced to wear European-style clothing and live in houses, the Indians gave up hunting, fishing and gathering their food and began farming. Men learned to tend crops and cattle, make tiles and tan hides. Women were taught to spin wool, weave blankets and make tallow candles.

After California came under control of the Mexican government in the 1830s, Mission holdings were secularized, and some of the land was sold off. The Mission padres, however, continued their religious work.

The Indians were allowed to leave, but many of them had become dependent on the Mission and found themselves unable to

return to their previous way of life. They could not afford to purchase land, nor did they have the experience to run ranchos when the Mission lands were carved up and sold. The Chumash population declined even more.

In 1839, the first bishop of Alta California selected the Santa Barbara Mission to become his home, thus ensuring that the site would not fall into disrepair—the fate that ruined many of California's missions.

Thanks to the efforts of civic-minded folk, the Mission is still framed by plenty of open space, and the buildings that have been constructed nearby are in keeping with the elegance of the Mission's design. After the 1925 earthquake, the Mission Fathers were forced to sell land immediately south of the Mission to raise the money needed for repairs. Local citizens raised $35,000 to purchase the land, which is now Mission Historical Park. The large lawn has become a favorite spot for photography students, picnickers, lovers who stroll hand-in-hand, and visitors from all over the world. The rose garden contains a hundred species of roses, and their fragrance wafts on the warm summer breeze.

Today, visitors come from all over the world to admire the architecture, examine the archival photos and artifacts, and read historic accounts of the purpose, intention and accomplishments of the Mission.

But the Mission is not just a tourist attraction; it serves as a worship site for an active parish community. A full schedule of masses is held, including an early morning weekday service that's a very special experience for the devout visitor. Dress appropriately, and maintain an attitude of reverence when visiting the Mission; it is, after all, a holy sanctuary.

Santa Barbara Architecture

2 miles one way

Bob Easton, editor of *Santa Barbara Architecture,* is a highly respected, highly opinionated architect. He helped us devise this walk through several classic Santa Barbara neighborhoods and has offered an architectural historian's perspective on the buildings he considers among Santa Barbara's finest examples of Spanish Colonial Revival and of the Craftsman Movement.

As Easton muses, "Architecture is history—use your imagination to bring it alive."

Directions: To reach the Mission by car, exit Highway 101 on Mission Street and head east to Laguna Street. Turn left and drive a few blocks to the Mission.

MTD: Line 22 Old Mission to the Mission.

The Walk: From the Mission steps, walk down to the fountain at the rose garden at Mission Historical Park. Pause a moment to admire the lovely block just in front of you—Plaza Rubio. It's a row of Spanish Colonial Revival homes designed by James Osborne Craig and Mary Craig and built in the 1920s.

The homes feature walled courtyards, simple arrangements and a sense of visual harmony. Architect Bob Easton notes, "The homes are absolute classics—nicely landscaped, there's a quiet, restful feeling about them. Allow your eye to wander and notice the details—iron gates, a lovely Spanish door, brick backyard patios."

After walking the length of Plaza Rubio and back, head across Laguna Street to the entrance of Junipero Plaza, marked by century-old sandstone arches and iron gates. Proceed through the block to Garden Street, pausing to ponder the design at 333, and continue through the arches on Garden Street. Turn right, then make an almost immediate left on Los Olivos. Stop here, at 232 Los Olivos, to examine a fine home built by George Washington Smith, Santa Barbara's preeminent architect of the Spanish Colonial Revival style. Notice the fine details—the brick courtyard and walkway, iron gate and bougainvillea-draped wall.

Return to Garden Street, turning right, and heading toward downtown through one of Santa Barbara's great Upper Eastside neighborhoods. Note the hitching posts built from Santa Barbara sandstone.

Continue to a group of five homes located on a palm-lined section of Garden Street, from 2050 to 2010. Known as "Crocker Row," these were once vacation homes built by the Crocker family of San Francisco. Notice

Sandstone and wrought iron grace each end of Junipero Plaza.

the window details and lovely Mission Revival style. Each was carefully positioned to enable residents of each house to enjoy ocean views.

Look for the larger-than-life statue of the dog in front of the corner house at 2010. It was placed there in the early 1900s in memory of a favorite pet left behind when the owners moved to California from Michigan. To the delight of many, the current residents often decorate it to coincide with holidays and special occasions. The dog has been seen wearing an Uncle Sam hat on the Fourth of July, a Pilgrim hat for Thanksgiving, and angel wings at Christmastime.

One of Santa Barbara's most visible residents, dressed in finery that changes to suit the holiday.

Continue down Garden, then turn left on Pedregosa to view the corner house of eclectic design (Bavarian/Spanish) then turn left on Laguna and examine the handsome bungalow at 1920 Laguna Street, representative of the Craftsman movement, circa 1910. Note the natural materials, low lines and rugged details, all characteristics of cottages like this one.

Return to Pedregosa, and continue heading east up the street, all the way past the DO NOT ENTER traffic sign. Turn right on Prospect for a view of a stunning house at 1741 Prospect. This beauty was built in 1911 by the noted architectural team of Greene and Greene, the only one of their houses built in Santa Barbara. The use of natural materials in the design is complemented by the landscaping and lovely gardens. Although it's partially hidden by shrubbery and built away from the street, it's worth craning your neck to get a good look. To examine this house from below, continue heading down Prospect (admire the view of the city below and the harbor beyond), and take a right on Valerio (note the sturdy stone garages), then a right on Olive Street where you'll hit the brick sidewalk. Look back up at the stately Greene and Greene design, and take in the natural beauty of this solid house and its graceful gardens, behind the Chinese archway.

Continue on the brick pathway, then turn left on Islay to view a number of cottage-style winter homes. Cross Laguna, staying on Islay as it jogs westward, then cross Garden Street, and turn left on Santa Barbara to 1721, to a most pleasing Victorian, a Queen Anne framed by two large palm trees. Continue south along Santa Barbara Street to the corner of Santa Barbara and Valerio. Pause to look at the view—a real mixture of architectural styles. On one corner, you'll see a Byzantine-style Christian tower, a Spanish Colonial dome, and a Frank Lloyd Wright-inspired, modern-looking, Unitarian Church with towering coral trees.

Turn left on Valerio up to Garden Street, then turn right; at 1624 Garden note the curious apartment court that looks like it's right out of one of the mystery novels written by the late, great Santa Barbara resident, Ross Macdonald.

At the corner of Arrellaga and Garden, pass through Alice Keck Park Memorial Garden, then turn right on Micheltorena. Stop at the corner to view another clash of styles; this time its Our Lady of Sorrows Catholic Church situated behind the neo-classical bungalow office building, with the Arlington Theatre spire in the background.

At this point in the walk, you can either head downtown via Anacapa, or return to the Mission by improvising a route on Garden, Santa Barbara or Anacapa Streets to Mission Street. These mansion-lined streets give an impressive view of stately old Santa Barbara.

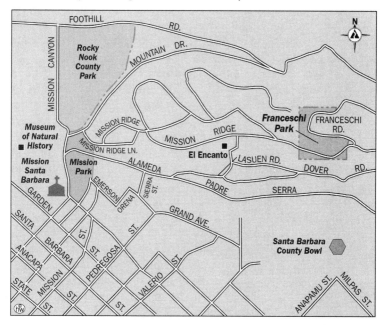

Use this map for Mission Santa Barbara, Santa Barbara Architecture, and America's Riviera Walks.

America's Riviera

From Mission to Franceschi Park is a 3.5 mile loop

On this walk, you'll visit a dream garden, pass a world-renowned resort and the breathtaking homes perched on "America's Riviera," discover a stair-step street, glimpse a hidden fountain and even walk along an Indian path. It's a walk you'll long remember, one that gives a very special view of Santa Barbara's best-kept secrets.

One destination is the beautiful garden of Italian botanist Francesco Franceschi, but on this walk, the journey itself is as much a reward as the destination. Don't get discouraged by the steep uphill at the beginning; the views and surprises are worth it.

This most certainly should not be the first walk attempted by newly arrived visitors. Directions are a bit tricky, the possibility for getting lost greater than the other city walks in this guide. Late afternoon is a nice time for this saunter to secret places.

Nearly a century ago, Italian botanist Francesco Franceschi wrote, "One can live for years in Santa Barbara, and never get tired of admiring the scenery of the mountains that rise between us and the rest of the world." This hidden walk will reveal not only the lovely scenery of Santa Barbara, but several spots of special interest that remain virtually unknown, even to long-time residents.

We'll explain more, but not until you start walking!

Directions: Exit Highway 101 on Mission Street and head east to Laguna Street. Turn left and drive a few blocks to the Mission, at the corner of Laguna and Los Olivos.

MTD: Line 22 Old Mission to the Mission.

The Walk: From the Mission steps, cross carefully at the crosswalk to the MTD stop. On the stone wall you'll find a plaque commemorating the 1806 construction of the Mission aqueduct by the padres and the Chumash, as well as a length of the aqueduct itself.

Follow the sidewalk as it curves right onto Alameda Padre Serra (or "APS" as locals call it). A sign reads "Scenic Drive"; another points the way to "El Encanto Hotel ½ mile." Stay with us, we'll lead you on a Scenic Walk to El Encanto—and to lots of places cars can't go.

At the sometimes busy and somewhat blind intersection of APS and Mission Canyon Road, cross APS to Mission Historical Park. Here you'll find the old Mission pottery building. Pick up the dirt path leading rightward and uphill past the old Mission reservoir site and a California Historical Landmark. just steps away uphill is the Mission's grist mill and

Santa Barbara's stair-step streets offer surprises in America's Riviera.

another reservoir site. Follow the dirt-and-railroad-tie path as it leads upward through oak-, cactus- and brush-dotted slopes. Crosses atop churches and the tops of palms dominate the skyline from this viewpoint.

The path soon intersects a stone staircase. A right down the stairs leads back to APS, but you head left, climbing a few stairs to Mission Ridge Road. Walk 50 yards to the signed intersection of Mission Ridge Road and Ridge Lane, stay on Ridge Lane and begin a slight ascent past some classic Santa Barbara homes.

The Riviera, one of Santa Barbara's most beautiful spots, affords grand views of the city, harbor and Channel Islands beyond. When a state teachers college campus was established on the Riviera in 1909, a number of large Mediterranean-style homes were built; gardens were planted, a streetcar line was established and immigrant stonemasons were hired to fashion the local stone into the walls, hitching posts and stairsteps that remain to this day.

At the intersection of Mission Ridge and Ridge Lane, join Mission Ridge right; continuing on your walk, you'll see Marymount School on your left. Walk past the Riviera office complex on your right. At the corner of Alvarado Place and Mission Ridge is the El Encanto Hotel; visit it on your return.

Continue just above the El Encanto, smug with the satisfaction of knowing that you've already completed more than half the climb. About when the houses run out, examine the grand view to your right, and beyond the eucalyptus trees to your left, the home of Dr. Francesco Franceschi. Keep following Mission Ridge Road to 1510 on your left. Don't turn up the private drive, but pick up the trail at a multi-trunked eucalyptus, and the Franceschi Park sign, zigzagging up-slope through the gardens. The 14-acre park site is all that remains of the 40 acres purchased by Dr. Emanual Orazio Fenzi, a horticulturist who moved here from his native Florence, Italy, in 1893. He changed his name to Francesco Franceschi, built the redwood house, which he dubbed "Montarioso" (airy mountain), and dreamt of establishing a model botanic garden on the then-barren, boulder-strewn spot. Although his grand plans fell somewhat short, he managed to introduce some 330 species to the area, and identified and catalogued 600 native species. He is sometimes remembered as the man who introduced the zucchini to America.

Civic leader Pearl Chase was instrumental in preserving the mansion and establishing the park; today's restoration efforts are being led by the Pearl Chase Society, the Santa Barbara County Horticultural Society and the Friends of Franceschi. After decades of politicking, the city now seems committed to a full restoration of the Franceschi house.

After you've enjoyed the park, return to Mission Ridge Road and descend to 1445, then follow the guardrail a hundred feet to a stone staircase, descending it to a cement walkway that heads south/southeast. This path soon splits; the left fork tunnels under oaks, but you turn right and continue downhill. Stop a moment to enjoy commanding views of the harbor and the city. Continue on the stone stairway and descend to Dover Road.

Go right on Dover a short block to a three-way junction. The upper road, Lasuen, leads to El Encanto; the middle road dead-ends in a lovely landscaped turnaround. You descend on Paterna Road, walking on the sidewalk on the right side of the street past stone walls and admire the lovely homes. Pay homage to Kermit and all his friends at the stone grotto, and continue on as Paterna Road meets and joins Lasuen, and you continue on the latter road. You'll soon spy the red sidewalk leading up to El Encanto Hotel.

The red sidewalk leads to a gorgeous lily pond, then to the entrance of El Encanto. Read the words by Henry Van Dyke on a sign above the door:

The lintel low enough to keep out pomp and pride. The threshold high enough to turn deceit aside; the doorband strong enough from robbers to defend, This door will open at a touch to welcome every friend.

Either continue along Lasuen a short block, or descend from the entrance of El Encanto to the corner of Lasuen and Alvarado. Join the asphalt path that leads diagonally to Riviera Park Research and Communication Center. Here you'll find a colonnade and a courtyard with a

beautiful pool. At the end of the Riviera complex is the Riviera Theatre. Notice the Chumash sculpture: a man with a pipe, a woman grinding acorns in a bowl, as well as two shields, one with an ax, one with an arrow.

From the Riviera Theatre, take the stairs to the lower parking lot, then cut across the lot to the exit at APS. Cross APS to the sidewalk, turn right, and walk 100 feet, looking left for a concrete stairway with steel pipe handrails. Descend the stairs, follow a cement path, then drop down another dozen stairs to short, steep Sierra Street, which might just as well be located in San Francisco, judging from its incline. Enjoy the neighborhood, and head for the end of the street at Grand. Go right. Almost immediately, at Orena Street, Grand splits. Take the lower road to its end at Plaza Bonita, where a Mission Revival neighborhood is complemented by a restful fountain complete with fish pond, waterlilies, and stone benches.

Double-back a few steps to Orena, and head down two short, steep blocks to Emerson Avenue. Go right one-half block to Padre. You can see Mission Historical Park, but don't head for it just yet; one more secret awaits your discovery.

Turn left on Padre, walking the sidewalk on the right side of the street. Look right, between 421 and 417 Padre Street, for the secret public paseo marked by four stone stairs and a handrail. Local legend has it that this passageway was part of an "Indian pathway" that led from the Mission to the Presidio. The path ends at Plaza Rubio, bringing you face-to-face with the fountain and the rose garden in the foreground, the Mission in the background. Linger awhile to enjoy the garden, then head back to the Mission.

Bungalow Haven

1 mile round trip

The Arts and Crafts Movement and its most prolific architectural expression—the bungalow—flourished in Santa Barbara during the first two decades of the 20th century. The movement was dedicated to promoting and preserving age-old handcraftsmanship at the dawn of the machine age. Arts and Crafts aficionados embraced the bungalow as the kind of house that best expressed their philosophy. In addition, many middle-class Americans, Santa Barbarans included, who had only a passing acquaintance with the kind of Arts and Crafts philosophy expressed in Gustav Stickley's *Craftsman* magazine, were attracted to the bungalow for more practical reasons: its modest cost, open floor plan and compelling simplicity.

In California, the Arts and Crafts movement and the building of bungalows peaked between the years of 1906 and 1914, lost ground during World War I (1914 to 1918), struggled and slowly faded out during the 1920s. In Santa Barbara, the city's 1925 earthquake hardly harmed the sturdily built little homes, but hastened the bungalow's demise by ushering in an era of municipally mandated emphasis on Spanish Revival architecture.

Northern California locales that experienced bungalow mania included San Francisco, Berkeley, and various East Bay communities. In Southern California, major bungalow building took place in Los Angles and in what were then two nature-blessed resort towns—Pasadena and Santa Barbara.

Santa Barbara Arts and Crafts artisans produced fabulous earthenware pottery, tooled leatherwork, and furniture with Spanish and Asian influences. Elizabeth Eaton Burton made marvelous lampshades of hammered copper with seashells and sold her wares nationwide via her successful mail order catalog.

Robert Wilson Hyde, the craftsman most closely associated with Santa Barbara's bungalow district, built a couple of houses on the corner of Salsipuedes and Victoria streets in 1910. Hyde's specialty was the creation of made-to-order commemorative books (guest books, wedding registers, etc.) and illuminated manuscripts, beautifully bound volumes that resembled something the monks of the Middle Ages produced.

Santa Barbara's bungalows are scattered eastside, westside, and all around the town, but only one neighborhood with a concentration of bungalows remains reasonably intact from the period. The city's bungalow district is bounded by Micheltorena Street on the north, Anapamu Street on the south, Garden Street on the east and Alta Vista Street on the west.

In recent years, the historic preservation movement has championed

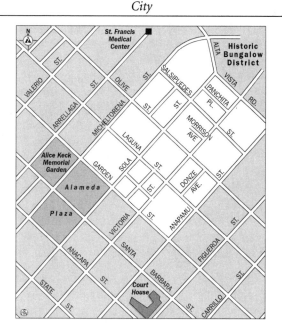

the humble bungalow with a resultant huge surge of public interest in the warm, accessible style. Santa Barbara's bungalow owners have formed a neighborhood association that seeks to educate the public about the city's Arts and Crafts heritage and to preserve the remaining examples of these wonderful homes.

The Craftsman neighborhood faces enormous pressure from fast-buck developers eager to tear down the historic bungalows (often small homes on relatively large lots) and construct condos.

Acknowledgement of the city's Arts and Crafts influences is long overdue. Oddly, this compelling period is skipped over by local historians, who seem eager to jump from the Victorian and early resort eras to the 1925 earthquake, without examining the first two decades of the 20th century. So, too, has the humble bungalow been overlooked by area historians, architects and politicos, often eager to promote every kind of strange structure from English manor houses to Italian villas, from Spanish castles and French châteaux to Spanish castles.

This walk explores the core of Santa Barbara's historic bungalow district, located just a few blocks from busy State Street, yet a world apart. Imagine Model Ts instead of SUVs in the narrow driveways; friendly neighbors still wave to you from their porches of yesteryear.

Directions: From Highway 101 in Santa Barbara, exit on Carrillo Street and drive about 8 blocks to Garden Street and turn left. Proceed north 4 blocks. Look for street parking on Garden Street between Sola

A lovingly restored bungalow, one of the many charms of this historic neighborhood.

and Micheltorena streets. Begin this walk on the east side of Garden Street at the signed Park East bungalow court.

Before beginning your bungalow walk, survey the inviting community parks located to the west of Garden Street. Look for grassy areas for picnics and play, and note that wonderful playground for children called Kid's World. Enticing paths lead through Alice Keck Park Memorial Garden, a lovely collection of botany surrounding a lily pond complete with turtles and colorful fish.

The Walk: Stroll past the tidy little bungalows in the city's best preserved Craftsman court. Turn left at the end of the court and walk past some Spanish-style units to Micheltorena Street.

Go right and saunter past bungalows on the south side of the street while staring across the street at some ugly 1960s-style apartment buildings. When you reach the Riviera Market, cross the street, locate the walkway between 425 and 429 Micheltorena and follow it into another Craftsman court of a half-dozen bungalows. When you emerge at a driveway, go right and head to Olive Street. Turn right again, walk past a few more bungalows, their porches nearly touching the sidewalk.

Continue on Olive past Micheltorena and turn left at the first opportunity onto De la Vista. The houses (90 percent bungalows) on this block are oriented to capture the ocean vistas promised in the street name. At Salsipuedes Street, turn right and descend a short block to Sola Street, another well-preserved street in the midst of Bungalow Haven. Continue to Alta Vista Street and descend a block to Victoria Street.

Detour left on Victoria for a block along a rare divided residential street to its end. Double-back past the Craftsman houses to Alta Vista, then continue another block to Panchita Place and turn right. Admire the well-preserved bungalows on this block-long street, turn left on Sola Street, then left again on Salsipuedes Street.

Descend steeply past a number of the so-called Sears houses (ordered from the famed catalog, shipped by rail to the Santa Barbara train station and assembled, often by their owners). Look for three Craftsman houses at the corner of Victoria and Salsipuedes streets. The one at the southwest corner at 1235 and the handsome one at 1225 were built about 1911 by the artist Robert Hyde, renowned for his illuminated manuscripts. Even today, old-time Santa Barbarans refer to each of them as "the Hyde house."

Turn right (west) on Victoria Street and walk half a block to Morrison Avenue, a completely intact cul-de-sac of bungalows, well worth a short detour. Continue another half-block to Olive Street and turn right, north. After a block, turn left on Sola Street and walk two more blocks to Garden Street, where you began your exploration.

Salsipuedes Street

For a look at the real city, walk Salsipuedes Street, just six blocks from State Street but a world apart. The two-mile long street was named in the mid-19th century for the swamp at the foot of it, and the impassable quagmire the street became after winter rains.

"*Sal si puedes,*" Spanish-speaking locals, warned: "Get out if you can" or "Escape if you can."

Begin at the north end of Salsipuedes at Micheltorena Street and head south, past some handsome Craftsman cottages. Three blocks along, Salsipuedes deadends at Anapamu Street. Cut through Santa Barbara High School, descend three blocks from the basketball courts to the baseball fields and rejoin Salsipuedes at Canon Perdido.

Salsipuedes' character abruptly shifts from the residential to the recreational—Girls Inc. of Greater Santa Barbara and the pool, playground and picnic area of Ortega Park—then to the commercial. Next comes the youth center of Casa de la Raza, the organization that successfully spearheaded the drive to honor the late labor leader César Chavez with a Santa Barbara street name—which turned out to be a segment of Salsipuedes.

Walk under the freeway, continuing the pilgrimage. The street leads past the DoubleTree Hotel and ends at Cabrillo Boulevard. Salsipuedes is a strange combination of tidiness and unseemliness, the past and the present, a street every bit as contradictory as Santa Barbara itself.

Santa Barbara Botanic Garden
Easton Trail

1 to 3 miles round trip

Nestled in the rugged landscape of Mission Canyon, the Santa Barbara Botanic Garden is truly a treasure, a living museum. Miles of soft pathways leading through California's ecosystems allow quick getaways from city life.

The garden, home to more than 1,000 species of native trees, shrubs, flowers and grasses, is a place to linger and learn.

Founded in 1926, this enclave devoted to the display, protection and research of native species has grown from its original 13 acres to its present size of 65 acres. Ecosystems represented included meadows, desert, chaparral, woodland, arroyo, and several others.

This is one of the few locations in the Southern California where a coast redwood forest has been successfully planted. These magnificent trees, located on the flat streambed along Mission Creek, provide a shady retreat with their canopied limbs and massive trunks.

The many floral life zones provide shelter for a number of species of wildlife, among them several dozen birds, amphibians and reptiles. Keep your eyes open for mammals, ranging from the California pocket mouse to mule deer.

Among the ongoing programs offered by the garden are lectures,

One of Santa Barbara's most ardent environmentalists, Robert Easton.

docent-led tours, field trips to other gardens, classes and workshops. A herbarium, library, year-round nursery and well-stocked garden bookstore are also attractions to plant lovers.

Easton Trail honors the late Robert Easton, a fourth-generation Californian, fine writer of California-themed books, and long-time conservationist, who worked diligently to protect the South-Central Coast and the Santa Barbara backcountry.

Directions: From Highway 101 in Santa Barbara, exit on Mission Street and head east to Laguna Street. Turn left and, keeping the Santa Barbara Mission on your left, you'll soon join Mission Canyon Road. When you reach a stop sign at Foothill Road, turn right, then make an almost immediate left back onto Mission Canyon Road. At a distinct V-intersection, keep right on Mission Canyon Road and follow it nearly to road's end, where you'll find the Santa Barbara Botanic Garden. Park in the garden's lot. There is a fee to enter the garden.

MTD: Field Trip, summer service only.

The Walk: From the garden's main entrance, as you pass the entry kiosk and approach the bookstore, turn left on the path near the cactus exhibit and head down into Mission Canyon. The buckwheat-bedecked trail descends into an arroyo ecosystem full of toyon and lemonade berry. Side trails lead to the garden's manzanita section.

The trail drops to the bottom of Mission Canyon, crosses Mission Creek and reaches an intersection with Easton Trail. Follow Easton Trail as it climbs moderately up the west wall of the canyon. Watch for some pieces of adobe pipe; these are 200-year-old remnants of the Santa Barbara Mission waterworks system.

Easton Trail descends to the garden's island section. Here you can marvel at the wonders of evolution, at how the Channel Islands plant species have evolved differently from their mainland cousins.

Joining Canyon Trail, you'll proceed up Mission Canyon, which is no planted garden, but a natural oak-sycamore woodland that was thriving long before Europeans arrived at California's shores.

The trail crosses over the top of Mission Creek Dam, built to hold water for the mission located about two miles below the dam. From the dam, a trail loops around a redwood grove. Planted 60 years ago, the redwoods are doing nicely in the cool canyon.

Now join one of the trails ascending out of the canyon to the main part of the garden. Enjoy the wide meadow and its multitude of flora with identification tags, then make your way back to the garden bookstore and trailhead.

Parma Park Natural Area
Parma Fire Road, Rowe Trail

2.5 mile loop through park with 300-foot elevation gain;
longer options available

With more than 200 acres, Parma Park Natural Area is both Santa Barbara's largest undeveloped open space and its best-kept secret. Sycamore Creek, Coyote Creek and several seasonal watercourses flow through the park, a mosaic of wooded canyons and brushy slopes.

The Parma family arrived in Santa Barbara in the 1870s and soon opened a grocery store on State Street and purchased acreage in the then-wild foothills, where they raised goats. A hundred years later the family donated their still very-much-undeveloped land to the city for a nature preserve.

Don't expect any of the usual park amenities—restrooms, water or parking lots. Trails and junctions are unsigned—by some accounts intentionally. The park has numerous steep side trails and paths that seem to start nowhere and end short of any conceivable destination. It's easy to imagine the park's maze of a trail system was actually developed by the goats that grazed these slopes a century ago.

First-time visitors should stick to the park's two main trails. One climbs an open slope to a vista point, where the hiker is rewarded with excellent views of Santa Barbara, the coastline, the Channel Islands and the wide blue Pacific. A second path lets you loop back to the trailhead by way of a lovely oak woodland.

For a day of mellow family hiking, pair the loop through Parma Park described below with a jaunt in the nearby Santa Barbara Botanic Garden, where the 5 miles of trail are signed, the plants are labeled and you'll find water, snacks, restrooms, and plenty of parking.

Directions: From Highway 101 in Montecito, a few miles downcoast from Santa Barbara, exit on Olive Mill Road and drive north. At a junction in 0.5 mile, you'll continue north, now on Hot Springs Road, for another 0.5 mile to East Valley Road (192)and turn left. After a short time, this road continues west under the name of Sycamore Canyon Road to a junction. Sycamore Canyon Road heads south but you continue west on Stanwood Drive and, 3 miles from where you first turned onto East Valley Road, you'll spot a turnout for parking on the right side of the road and a sign for Parma Park.

To reach the Santa Barbara Botanic Garden, continue west on 192 which, to confuse you, undergoes three more name changes (Mission

Ridge Road to Mountain Drive to Foothill Road). Two miles from the park, you'll reach a stop sign and a signed junction with Mission Canyon Road. Turn right and drive 0.75 mile to the garden entrance on the left side of the road.

The Walk: Walk north past the park entrance sign and vehicle gate and across an old stone bridge. Look for a cluster of picnic tables on the right and join unsigned Rowe Trail, which descends to a branch of Sycamore Creek, crosses it and climbs east on a parallel course above Stanwood Drive.

The path widens, then bends left to top a minor ridge, where there's a vista point. Sit at the picnic table and enjoy the great view, then join Parma Fire Road, which makes a rolling descent to a woodland. Cross Sycamore Creek and close the loop.

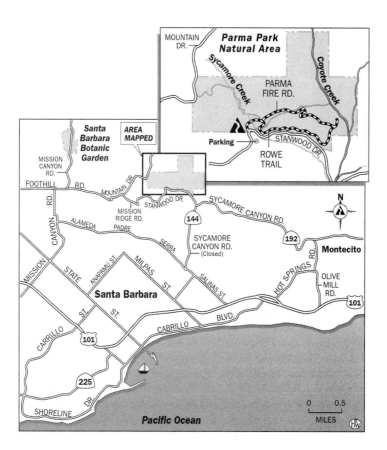

State Street

From Arlington Theater to Paseo Nuevo is 8 blocks one-way

State Street has historically been the major corridor of commerce in Santa Barbara. Banks, medical buildings, hotels and shopping areas have been clustered on the street for more than a century. Today, the number of attractive shops, inviting ambience, and the historic feel, attract shoppers and strollers from around the world to this street.

Stretching the length of the city, State Street—Santa Barbara's Main Street—has different moods at different times of the day. On cool mornings, a stroll down the shady street reveals the city just waking up. Traffic is light; sidewalk cafés, coffeehouses and bakeries serve up their best cuppa java to early-rising tourists and impatient commuters; shop owners sweep the sidewalk and tidy their storefronts.

By mid-afternoon, the street bustles in the bright sunlight. The air filled with a dozen different languages as visitors shop the day away. In the evenings, diners and film-goers replace shoppers on the sidewalk. Theaters turn on their neon signs, and the whole street takes on new life. Restaurants open their doors, and the hippest clubs in town attract decked-out dancers for a night-on-the-town. The street becomes a cruise strip, music blares from car stereos, and everybody checks out everybody else.

Open-air shopping paseos on State Street include Victoria Court, La Arcada, San Marcos and El Paseo, which offer an array of unique shops; goods range from tourist T-shirts to one-of-a-kind art objects. Restaurants within strolling distance offer diverse dining experiences— everything from Tex-Mex to California Cuisine, from funky coffeehouse fare to elegant gourmet meals.

Downtown State Street—not to be confused with upper State Street, which has a commercial district and motel row of its own, or with lower State Street, also called Old Town—is the commercial heart of the city, an interesting mix of old and new. It's still possible to discover a few mom-and-pop shops, but rising rents and redevelopment are forcing many to relocate or go out of business altogether. Some bemoan the loss of distinctive historic buildings and small businesses, while others advocate modernization as necessary for the city's economic health. Without a doubt, State Street is changing and at a much more rapid pace than ever before. Time will tell if the street will keep its charm, or grow to resemble the mini-malled and overdeveloped shopping strips of suburban Los Angeles.

The Arlington Theatre, where this walk begins, houses a magnificent pipe organ that has been restored by a group of hardworking volunteers.

Shopping is the thing on State Street.

The Santa Barbara Theatre Organ Society sponsors an annual concert series; inquire at the Arlington ticket agency.

Directions: Begin at the Arlington Theatre, 1317 State Street.

MTD: Downtown/Waterfront Shuttle.

The Walk: The Arlington Theatre is an architectural gem. Built in the early 1930s on the site of the old Arlington Hotel, it is an excellent example of Spanish Colonial Revival design, created by architect Joseph Plunkett. The murals on the walls, tile work, graceful columns, wrought-iron details and heavy, painted beams combine to give this building a Mediterranean style; it was designated a city landmark in 1975.

In a world of mall theaters that are little more than warehouses with screens, its a pleasure to view a movie or attend a concert staged in this grand picture palace with its distinctive spire-topped roof. Inside, make-believe stars twinkle on the curved ceiling above an extravagantly decorated performance house that resembles a Mediterranean village.

Head downtown (south) on State Street, and turn right on Victoria to see a large tile mural applied to the side of a building that houses a supermarket. The mural depicts Santa Barbara County history from Chumash culture to the space age.

Head back to State and wander into Victoria Court. Several shops, restaurants and services are offered along the street and within the winding paths and courtyards.

Note the Granada Building on the east side of State; it's an eight-story office building and theater complex. It was constructed without windows on three sides because developers fully expected that one day State Street would be lined with similar such high-rises. But that was just before the devastating 1925 earthquake, and the subsequent action by the city council banning all commercial buildings above four stories high. So the Granada remains the tallest building in Santa Barbara, and one of the few that wasn't heavily damaged in the earthquake. Judge for yourself if you think the Granada is distinctive looking or merely sticks out like a sore thumb.

Located in the 1100 block of State Street are the former Woolworth Building, which housed the local five-and-dime until the late 1980s, and the San Marcos building, built in 1869 to serve as the city's first secondary school. It was later converted into a hotel and today it houses an array of shops, restaurants and offices.

During the 1925 earthquake, the San Marcos lost its two top floors but the lower floors survived intact. The ornamental façade was added after the quake. Stroll into the paseo to enjoy a bit of old California maintained or not depending upon the occupancy of the here-today-gone-tomorrow restaurant building.

The Santa Barbara Museum of Art's proud building, located at State and Anapamu, formerly housed the city's post office; it was converted in the thirties, then remodeled in 1983. It's a handsome building, best seen from across the street to fully appreciate the classic Italian design. The Art Museum gives way to La Arcada Court, a popular paseo that features tempting restaurants and a collection of art galleries and lovely shops. The dolphins, located within the arcade, are popular with parents who like to photograph their children sitting atop them. They were created by local artist Bud Bottoms, who also designed the dolphin statue located at the foot of Stearns Wharf.

At 1029 State Street, two plaques mark the changing face of the spot. Located here first was an adobe owned by the Orella family; in 1927, the Copper Coffee Pot was built. Another restaurant has taken over the building and modified it somewhat, but the lovely balcony and patio area still remain.

Continue strolling down State Street, visiting the shops that suit your fancy, noting the many examples of Colonial Revival architecture with red-tiled roofs, arches, wrought-iron details, the use of Greek columns, colorful awnings, and second-floor balconies.

El Paseo, designed by architect James Osborne Craig, is a cluster of small shops, offices and café situated next to the historic Casa de la Guerra. Wander "The Street of Spain" and note the red-tiled roofs, white walls and classic iron grillwork, tiles, landscaping, and beautiful fountain.

Return to State Street and continue your exploration stopping to enjoy Paseo Nuevo, an open-air shopping center with a graceful circular plaza, upscale chain stores, boutique shops and restaurants, as well as a theater complex, performing arts center and gallery of contemporary art.

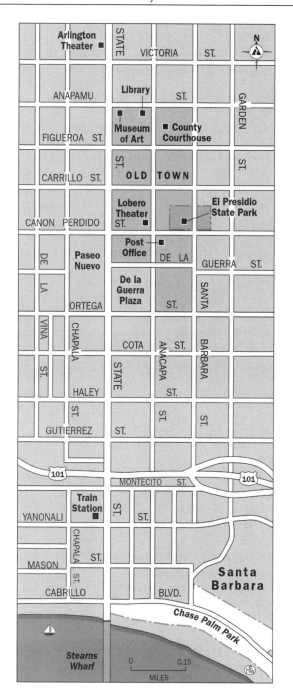

Paseo Santa Barbara

14 blocks round trip

Enjoy a leisurely stroll of Santa Barbara's scenic paseos with this off-the-beaten-path adventure. Passage through the paseos offers an intimate view of Santa Barbara and the discovery of some unique shopping areas, restaurants, and historical sites.

It's no accident that Santa Barbara is so easily accessible on foot; the city has been carefully designed with the pedestrian in mind. The tradition dates back to the Presidio days, and it continues more than two centuries later.

The term paseo refers to a pedestrian lane or walkway. Since the area has been extensively redeveloped in recent years, city agencies have attempted to continue the tradition of the paseos, even with the addition of multi-level city parking lots.

The most attractive paseos are graceful, charming and romantic, lined with lovely gardens, interesting shops and outdoor cafés. Others, however, are little more than alleyways, obviously requiring attention before they can properly be termed paseos. But taken as a whole, the paseo system of walkways gives a human-sized quality and dimension to Santa Barbara's downtown streets.

The fun—and the challenge—is to use the city's paseos, not State, Anacapa or Chapala streets, except when absolutely necessary. Use caution in parking lots and when crossing streets.

Directions: Park in the city lot on Ortega, between State Street and Anacapa Street.

MTD: Downtown/Waterfront Shuttle with many stops on State Street.

The Walk: Our paseo walk begins on the north side of Ortega street, between the Santa Barbara News-Press Building and the interesting building at the corner of Anacapa and Ortega, long-ago site of the county courthouse. Walk through the News-Press parking lot past the loading dock, and angle left toward the flower beds to de la Guerra Plaza Street, the tiny street that borders historic de la Guerra Plaza.

Since the early 1800s, de la Guerra Plaza has been Santa Barbara's ceremonial gathering spot and festival site. Each year, during the city's Old Spanish Days celebration, the plaza becomes a *mercado*, or marketplace.

The News-Press Building that anchors the plaza was designed by architect George Washington Smith in 1922. The newspaper, once owned by the *New York Times* now locally owned by Wendy McCaw, is the oldest daily journal published in Southern California. A number of distinctive shops and restaurants line the perimeter of the plaza.

Also located on de la Guerra Plaza is Santa Barbara's City Hall, a small, graceful building of Spanish Colonial Revival style. Built in 1923, it somehow survived the 1925 earthquake, and served as a model during the city's rebuilding efforts. Today, it's a common sight to view news crews as they set up their taping sessions and interview city officials in front of the building.

From the east side of plaza, cross de la Guerra Street, and head across to "The Street in Spain" in lovely El Paseo. This is the gateway to one of Santa Barbara's most unique and historic spots: wander the narrow walkways, peaceful courtyard and interesting collection of shops, art galleries and studios.

Be sure to examine the tiles that tell the story of Santa Barbara, and visit Casa de la Guerra museum and shop, where you may look at interesting vintage photos of de la Guerra family, and early views of Santa Barbara's first mansion. This was the site of the grand fandango (the wedding celebration of the youngest de la Guerra daughter) that Richard Henry Dana wrote about in *Two Years Before the Mast*.

As you make your way through the labyrinthine corridors, you'll end up in the parking lot across the street from the post office. In front of you is the tiny building occupied by Madame Rosinka, the Palm Reader. Head over to the paseo located between El Centro Building and the west side of the Lobero Theatre. Check the coming attractions kiosk, and then walk along the brick walkway where a red hibiscus blooms delightfully during the summer months.

Follow the beige tiles, then angle west (left) behind Santa Barbara Bank & Trust and the Masonic Temple. Curving right, you'll emerge between a Spanish-style row of shops and the Bank of Montecito, coming face-to-face with a lovely Monterey Revival-style building, and its next door neighbor, the Hill-Carrillo Adobe on Carrillo Street. Cross the street; from this vantage point, look back at the ornate Mediterranean designs on the Masonic Temple.

Walk along the eastern (right) side of the adobe, keep on a northward path, and head past a row of junipers. Ascend the stairsteps leftward, then continue north behind the restaurants and shops. Pause at the sycamore-shaded benches to examine the view. You'll spot distinctive buildings with red-tiled roofs, palm trees, and the Santa Ynez mountains in the distance. The sharp-eyed will note the Courthouse tower.

Cross Figueroa Street, jog to the right just a bit and head into La Arcada. Inside, enjoy the casual ambience of this classic paseo, its fountains, flower pots, bright flags and tiles. Linger awhile at the shops, art galleries and outdoor eateries.

Walk past the back entrance of the Museum of Art, alongside the Main Library, where you'll examine the abstract sculpture of lacquered steel entitled *Intermezzo* by Anthony Caro. Walk between the museum and the library toward Anapamu Street, cross the street and head a few steps to the right. Pass through the bougainvillea-draped walkway across Anapamu Street, skirting the parking lot and bearing left, angling toward two ersatz Corinthian columns, and turning left to State Street.

(Do note that the return trip of the paseo walk is more challenging than the first half, but be dogged. The city has not been as faithful to the paseo concept on the west side of State Street as it has been on the east. The persistent paseo walker must detour a few times to Chapala Street.)

Cross State Street, heading right into Victoria Court, where you'll explore shops and restaurants, and a pleasant ambience.

Walk to the back of Victoria Court, to the sidewalk fronting the park-

ing lot and turn left by the tiny post office. Stay on the paseo to Anapamu Street; turn right to examine the wall that hides the parking lot. It offers two points of interest: a snoozing cat sculpture and a tile mural explaining the meaning of the Chumash word *anapamu.*

Cross Anapamu Street. When the Karpeles Manuscript Library is open (Wednesday through Sunday 1 P.M. to 4 P.M.), stop in and examine its priceless letters and documents penned by historic figures including Napoleon, George Washington, Albert Einstein, Abraham Lincoln and King Henry VIII. When the library is open, continue straight through to the next

Manuscripts illuminate understanding at the Karpeles Library.

paseo; if closed, head right to Chapala Street at Anapamu, then make the first left back into the parking lot.

Pass through Paseo Figueroa, then a parking lot with the Transit Center on your right. The paseo ends again at Carrillo; head right to Chapala, then left and left again into the bricked parking lot and paseo. Don't miss the tile compass embedded in the walkway. Reorient yourself and head eastward, noting the elaborate parking structure on the right, the nicely landscaped storefronts on the left.

Across the street, you'll see what must be one of the most beautiful supermarkets ever built.

Crossing Canon Perdido, you'll enter Santa Barbara's newest shopping area, Paseo Nuevo. In the mix of specialty shops and architectural details between Canon Perdido and Ortega streets, don't miss the Santa Barbara Contemporary Arts Forum.

To get there, take a right just past the large semicircular gathering place and twin fountains. Head toward Chapala Street, then ascend the tiled, multi-pattern Grand Staircase (you could take the elevator, but, hey, you're a walker). At the top of the stairs, head right into the 4,600-square-foot forum, which houses two exhibit spaces, a media library, shop and bookstore.

Across the way from CAF is the Center Stage Theater, a state-of-the-art, community-access theater that offers flexible seating arrangements for audiences up to 150. Check the box office for a schedule of performances.

Head back down the stairs, then meander through Paseo Nuevo to Ortega Street, and your starting point.

Tree City, USA

IT's NOT ALWAYS easy living in a city that so cherishes its trees. You're in for a fight—not to mention front-page headlines in the local press—if you want to cut down a beloved eucalyptus that threatens to crush your home or have concern that a bunya-bunya's pointy cones make it a hazard for all who venture near.

This is a city where redwood groves and rare palms flourish; where visitors flock to gawk at an overgrown fig tree with gnarly roots—a tourist attraction for a century. Another Moreton Bay fig tree, which surely would have been felled elsewhere, instead became the centerpiece of a popular local restaurant. The International House of Pancakes currently occupies the spot.

But Santa Barbara's beloved trees have not always dominated the local landscape. Santa Barbara was all but tree-free, at least according to Mission founder Padre Junípero Serra, who described the future site of the city as "dismal and treeless" when he first saw it in 1782.

A hundred years later, Santa Barbara's urban forest grew mightily with the arrival of Dr. Augustus Boyd Doremus, a wealthy dentist who settled here to improve his failing health. He was attracted to the area because it reminded him of the French Riviera. Although doctors told him he might die in a short time, Doremus went on to become the Johnny Appleseed of Santa Barbara and lived another 55 years after his physicians' grave pronouncements.

Doremus purchased a barren half-block on east Anapamu Street and planted a glorious garden there. He and Dr. Francesco Franceschi, a horticulturalist noted for the introduction of many plants new to America, traded seeds, pods, and cones and brought the Eastside botanical splendor. Doremus is credited with planting the Italian stone pines that line Anapamu Street to this day. And the considerable plantings of Franceschi can still be seen in the Riviera park that bears his name.

At the dawn of the 20th century, Doremus was appointed to Santa Barbara's first park commission and placed in charge of park planning and planting. He planted the lawns and some 70 species of trees in Alameda Park, including the graceful feather palms that extend through the park and surrounding blocks. Doremus also appreciated native species: he was instrumental in adding oaks, California maples and toyon to the existing coast live oak and sycamores in Oak Park.

In 1911, the city of Santa Barbara, recognizing the need to professionally tend its trees, hired its first tree warden, "the guardian of the trees." Today, the full-time position is called city arborist and, for more than two decades, Dan Condon has held the job. The arborist's duties include overseeing both park and street trees, their maintenance, placement and replacement. "I don't consider myself an avid tree-hugger," states Condon, "but I love trees. I don't talk to trees and they don't talk to me. But I do consider myself a professional tree care advocate, and approach each tree with appreciation and respect."

Today, Santa Barbara's urban forest includes 230 different species of street trees and 300 different park trees. Number one is the jacaranda with some 2,000 individuals—all of which bloom in eye-pleasing color in May and June—before messily dropping their pretty lavender-blue petals shortly thereafter. Runners-up include 1,900 Queen palms, many of which are located on State Street and near the courthouse; 880 Mexican fan palms and 850 King palms. The most populous native under city stewardship is the coast live oak.

Some of the most rare trees include the chinaberry, the only specimen of which is located at the corner of Grand and Moreno, the Montezuma cypress located at Yanonali and Bath, and the Cigar Box trees that line east and west Gutierrez.

Every city block in Santa Barbara has a designated street tree. Olive Street's designated tree is obvious; others, however, are not. On Victoria Street, the once-designated pittosporum, all but annihilated by droughts of the 1980s and deluges of the 1990s, are being replaced by the street's new official tree, the ginkgo.

The city arborist's office occasionally functions as the tree police, approving or disallowing plans to plant the parkways that line city streets. Each month, the Street Tree Advisory Committee meets to ponder the fate of trees requested for removal or planting.

The trees of Santa Barbara are like so many residents here—a spectacular array of diverse individuals thriving in the mild climate, some who whisper, others who shout, all happy to put down roots in an environment conducive to growth.

Santa Barbara History and Culture

1 mile or so

Explore the exotic Santa Barbara County Courthouse, tour some of the first dwellings and structures in town, and visit several culturally significant sites, including a historic performing arts center, the Historical Museum, the public library with its art gallery, and the famed Museum of Art. Along the way, you'll have the chance to stop in lovely courtyards and stop to eat at any number of tempting restaurants.

This walk isn't much more than a mile but plan to spend the better part of a morning or afternoon; to really enjoy the sights demands lots of time and attention.

Admission to the Santa Barbara County Courthouse is free; docent-led tours are conducted Tuesday through Saturday at 2 P.M.; additional tours Wednesday and Friday at 10:30 A.M.; the observation tower closes at 4:45 P.M.

Free admission to the Santa Barbara Museum of Art every Thursday and the first Sunday of the month; closed on Monday; open Tuesday through Saturday 11 A.M. to 5 P.M., Thursday 11 A.M. to 9 P.M., Sunday noon to 5 P.M.

The Historical Museum is closed on Monday, open Tuesday through Saturday 10 A.M. to 5 P.M., Sunday 12 noon to 5 P.M.; free docent-led tours Wednesday, Saturday and Sunday at 1:30 P.M.; Gledhill Library open Tuesday through Friday 10 A.M. to 4 P.M.

Directions: This walk begins at the Santa Barbara County Courthouse, which occupies the entire 1100 block of Anacapa Street. Parking is available on the street (75-minute zone strictly enforced) or in the lot just behind the public library. Enter via Anacapa opposite the courthouse.

MTD: Downtown Waterfront Shuttle to Anapamu Street; walk two blocks east to the Courthouse. Also, Line 1 East/West connection.

The Walk: The huge, gleaming white stucco building topped with a red-tile roof is one of the most distinctive public structures in America. Visitors sometimes fail to realize that the Santa Barbara County Courthouse is not just a tourist attraction, but the building where all manner of government business takes place. As you wander through the tile- and wrought iron-adorned hallways, remember that marriage licenses and birth certificates are obtained here, grand juries assembled, voters registered, bankruptcies declared, arraignments held and prisoners sentenced.

The courthouse is an example of Spanish Colonial Revival architecture; it was built after the 1925 earthquake destroyed the previous

The Fourth of July celebration at the Courthouse draws thousands who proudly show their patriotic spirit.

masonry structure located on the same site. San Francisco architect William Mooser and his son were awarded the contract for the replacement building. The younger Mooser had lived in Spain and studied Moorish design; his background obviously influenced this project.

Time your visit to take a docent-led tour, or wander through the hallways on your own. Notice the grand ceiling design just above this entrance; it's a replica of one seen in a synagogue in Toledo, Spain. Be sure to stop in the second-floor mural room for an artistic overview of Santa Barbara history.

For the best view in town, head for the clock tower, El Mirador (take the elevator to the fourth floor). This observation deck, 85 feet above ground, gives you a panoramic view of the entire city. Compass points painted on the floor help visitors get oriented with Santa Barbara's sometimes confusing layout.

Head back down to the first floor, exit the courthouse and stroll around the grounds. You'll find arches carved with quotations from Virgil ("learn justice from this warning") and Coke ("reason is the life of the law"), tile murals—including one commemorating the visit of Queen Elizabeth and Prince Philip in 1983—and the so-called sunken garden, which is planted on the foundation area of the former courthouse building. The amphitheater is the site for annual summer celebrations, including an Independence Day concert and performances during the city's celebration of Old Spanish Days, known as Fiesta.

After strolling the grounds, make your way to Santa Barbara Street (parallel to Anacapa, the street behind the main courthouse entrance) and head south to continue the walk.

Stop at the tile plaque on the modern building at 1014 Santa Barbara Street. It's the former site of the Koury Market, a neighborhood market that was the "home of the five-cent sandwich."

Continue one more block down Santa Barbara Street to Canon Perdido and turn right. Here you'll find the next stop on the walk, El Presidio de Santa Barbara State Historic Park. The one-time Spanish military fortress was founded here in 1782, one of four such outposts in California, and is currently under reconstruction based on archeological excavations that have been conducted on the Presidio site since the mid-1960s.

Don't miss the ascetic room of a padre, an early kitchen, and other rooms typical of the Spanish colonization of the area two centuries ago. Take a stroll through El Presidio Chapel, a recreation of the city's first church. The Spanish artifacts on the altar and colorful wall paintings provide an interesting contrast to the building's simple exterior.

Stop in the park headquarters to view a display of artifacts found on

the Presidio site, and to read about the history of the Canedo Adobe, the former quarters for military officers, a private home, and even a Chinese laundry. The Santa Barbara Trust for Historic Preservation, now headquartered here, is responsible for the reconstruction and interpretation of the Presidio.

To continue the walk, keep heading south down Santa Barbara Street, stopping at the Rochin Adobe, the first parcel of land sold after the Presidio was dismantled. Anyone who has the slightest knowledge about Santa Barbara real estate prices will be astonished to know that the 1856 selling price of this 250-foot by 120-foot lot was originally $30. The house, which is privately owned and currently inhabited by descendants of the original family, is constructed of adobe bricks salvaged from the Presidio wall; painted wooden siding obscures the adobe, however.

At the corner of Santa Barbara Street and de la Guerra, stop in at the Santa Barbara Historical Museum. An original gas lamp that once stood on State Street is installed in the front of the museum. This eclectic collection of Santa Barbara-California memorabilia includes artists' renderings of missions and Santa Barbara buildings, a nineteenth-century wicker pony cart, a sacred Chinese shrine that was once a part of Santa Barbara's Chinatown, and sketches by Edward Borein, a renowned Western artist. The focus of one display is a Santa Barbara map, circa 1886; it's fun to try to conjure up an image of what the small town looked like back then.

The museum's research library, Gledhill Library, is located in the lovely courtyard area behind the museum. Its extensive collection of books, maps, photographs, genealogy charts, documents and oral history tapes is available to researchers. Historic photos on display provide a wondrous glimpse into Santa Barbara's past.

The walk continues on Santa Barbara Street, at the quiet grounds and lovely gardens of Casa Covarrubias, a historic adobe built for early Santa Barbara leaders in 1817. Today, the house, which has been designated a California Historic Landmark, serves as headquarters for Los Rancheros Visitadores.

Retrace your steps on Santa Barbara Street back to de la Guerra Street (in front of and then west of the Historical Museum). Note the tiles on buildings across the street that indicate the site of the original Presidio, and pause at 112-116 de la Guerra to view the lovely Mediterranean courtyard of the Meridian Studios. The stucco and brick studios were built in 1923 by the noted architect George Washington Smith. The historic Lugo adobe, built about 1830, stands at the end of the courtyard.

Dress-up days at the Presidio recreate the early Santa Barbara scene.

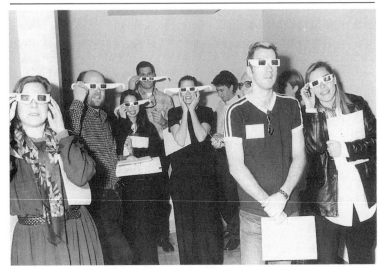

The Museum of Art attracts art-lovers with their own particular vision.

Cross the street to tiny Presidio Avenue, the oldest street in Santa Barbara. This is the site of the Guardhouse, commemorated by a tile plaque. Around the corner, read the framed proclamation of El Adobe de Miranda, once occupied by Captain John C. Frémont. Just across the way, stop at Presidio Gardens, the peaceful courtyard surrounded by law offices. With its koi pond, fountain and shaded gardens, it's a perfect spot for a rest or even a picnic lunch. Don't miss the graceful blue vases that stand atop the building outside the courtyard.

Return to de la Guerra, named for the first commandante of the Presidio, and turn right on Anacapa Street. You'll pass historic El Paseo shopping area on your left. Continue north on Anacapa, past the post office on your right. A commemorative marker noting the establishment of the Presidio on the site has been presented and placed at the top of the stairs by the Native Sons of the American West. The post office was built in 1937; its Art Deco design, with a Spanish influence, combine to make it a distinctive building.

Note the Lobero Theatre building at the corner of Canon Perdido and Anacapa. It is the second performing arts forum to stand on this site. In 1873, Italian immigrant Giuseppe "José" Lobero, realized his dream of building a grand opera house to rival those in his native land. Despite the fact that the theater stood in what at the time was considered a bad side of town, the 1,300-seat opera house flourished for more than a decade. But a small town like Santa Barbara could hardly support such an entertainment palace; it fell on hard times and eventual foreclosure. Lobero finally committed suicide in 1892, and the building was razed in 1922.

Local citizens raised nearly $200,000 to build a new theater, which opened in 1924. Miraculously, it was not damaged in the 1925 earthquake that devastated much of the city. In the years since its opening, the theater has hosted Hollywood's top stars. Today, the nonprofit Lobero Theatre Foundation manages the theater and hosts an array of performing artists from all over the world. The 600-seat Lobero is noted for its intimacy and elegant surroundings. Stop by the ticket office and check out the performance schedule.

Head back up Anacapa, noting the Courthouse clock tower on the right just a few blocks away. Stop to admire the four-story Lobero Building at 924 Anacapa; it was designed by noted San Francisco architect Julia Morgan, known for her work on the magnificent Hearst Castle. She also designed the ivy-covered brick Community Recreation Center building next door.

At this point in the walk, you have the option of returning to the Courthouse or continuing on to the art galleries of the public library and the Santa Barbara Museum of Art.

At the corner of Anacapa and Anapamu stands the Santa Barbara Public Library. Head west on Anapamu to the entrance, stopping first to admire the decorative arch that was once the main doorway. The figures are Aristotle and Plato; the crests surrounding the city's coat of arms are the shields of four of the world's great libraries: University of Bologna (Italy), Bibliothéque Nationale (France), University of Salamanca (Spain) and Oxford's Bodleian Library (England). Inside the library, the Faulkner Gallery showcases the work of local artists.

Continue west on Anapamu to State Street, turn left, and head up the steps to the Santa Barbara Museum of Art.

The museum houses the most extensive collection of art on the Central Coast. Whether your taste runs to antiquities, Asian art, French impressionism, or abstract expressionism, you're sure to find something you like in this impressive regional museum. Among the treasures in the permanent collection are *Brooklyn Bridge #7* by David Hockney and *Kneeling Caryatid* by Auguste Rodin.

Gallery tours, talks and special lecture series are regularly scheduled, as are classes and workshops for children and very popular art tours of destinations as diverse as Santa Fe, Moscow, and Istanbul. The museum bookstore features an interesting collection of art books, jewelry and gift items—and the restaurant is a hidden gem. Return to the Courthouse by heading east on Anapamu.

Old Town

From Old Town to Stearns Wharf is 1 mile

Called Old Town by the merchants, and Lower State by most locals, the section of State Street from Ortega to the ocean is lined with one-of-a-kind shops, eateries and a thriving local club scene. Boosters refer to the area as a "zesty mix of ethnic restaurants, hotels, offices and enticing specialty shops."

Oceanward of the freeway, lower Lower State has a marine emphasis—surf and swimwear shops, seafood restaurants. Just off lower Lower State are two not-to-be missed Santa Barbara sights: the Southern Pacific train station and the Moreton Bay Fig Tree.

A massive (by Santa Barbara standards) shopping-restaurant-time-share-condo complex known as La Entrada has long been pushed by a local property owner-developer. If built, this highly controversial development will completely change the character of lower State and the walker's approach to the coast.

Santa Barbara has long had the dubious distinction among California cities of being the last to remove traffic lights from its section of U.S. Highway 101. Removal of the lights meant construction of the cross-town freeway during the early 1990s. With the new, traffic-lightless highway, State Street was routed under the freeway and an underpass now links State Street's beach area with the downtown section.

State Street ends (or begins, if you prefer) at Stearns Wharf, at one time Santa Barbara's major "port of entry." In tandem with the wharf, State Street grew to become the community's main thoroughfare for commercial trade. Hotels were built to serve the shipping trade, and with the dawn of the Automobile Age, several dealerships were established. Most of these businesses have moved to other locations, but some of the distinctive buildings remain.

Directions: Park in the Ortega Street parking garage located between State Street and Anacapa Street.

MTD: Downtown/Waterfront Shuttle.

The Walk: Begin at the corner of State and Ortega, where buildings constructed nearly a century apart stand across the street from one another: Paseo Nuevo (circa 1990) on one side of the street, the Fithian Building (circa 1895) on the other. Before the 1925 earthquake, the Fithian Building was a three-and-a-half-story building, but its clock tower and top floor were severely damaged during the temblor and removed. Today, the building houses offices and a number of small businesses.

On Tuesday evenings the Certified Farmer's Market sets up on the

500 and 600 blocks, offering a tempting selection of healthful, locally grown produce.

Continue down State, exploring the eclectic selection of specialty shops, and depending on the time of day, don't miss two Santa Barbara institutions, both usually packed with hungry locals and hopeful visitors. For breakfast, it's Esau's (403 State) for the best pancakes in town, and for lunch and dinner, make way for Joe's Café (536 State). Check out the Moorish-looking building with the tower and the pedestrian arcade at 318 State near the freeway. Continue on State Street underneath Highway 101.

Bear right to the landmark Southern Pacific Railroad Depot, one of the last Mission Revival-style stations in California. As one turn-of-the-century railroad architect put it: "Give me neither Romanesque nor Gothic; much less Italian Renaissance and least of all English Colonial. This is California, give me Mission!" The depot was renovated recently and restored to its original coloration.

After admiring the station, which has been in active service since 1905, walk to Chapala Street and turn right to view another city landmark, the giant Moreton Bay fig tree. It has grown from a seedling planted in 1877 to its present size of over 70 feet tall with a 10-foot diameter trunk. It was once a major attraction, second only to the Mission, but since the freeway underpass opened it has attracted fewer visitors.

Return to State Street. Near the beach are surf and surfwear shops, cycle rental establishments and fish restaurants—everything you'd expect from a beach town. Walk back the way you came, return by the shuttle bus, or join one of the beachfront walks detailed in this guide.

To shop, perchance to dream, in Old Town Santa Barbara.

haley Street

A STROLL DOWN Haley, from downtown's State Street to the Eastside's Milpas Street, is a walk from the world of the tourist to the real world; just steps from Haley is a light-industrial neighborhood dotted with a few community-supported residence hotels, along with auto repair and body shops, tile, glass and plumbing suppliers, and a once-somewhat notorious nightlife.

At a time when many neighborhoods in Santa Barbara are subject to massive and sudden governmental (re)development, it's refreshing to witness natural, evolutionary change that quietly and creatively serves the needs of those who live and work here. A diverse group of entrepreneurs is slowly transforming the area sometimes known as SoCo (South of Cota Street). Haley surprises. You might expect to cruise over for some homemade tamales or chicken *mole*, but you might be surprised at the opportunity to shop in a tony boutique (TakaPuna, relocated here from Los Angeles), or relax over a double decaf latte.

Nearby you'll also find the offices of graphics designers, an artist's studio, a gourmet sausage shop, an upscale bakery, plus more surprises along the way. Located about halfway between State and Milpas, the coffeehouse Muddy Waters features an ever-changing gallery of art.

Not to be missed is La Tolteca, located at 614 East Haley, a Santa Barbara institution since 1952. The restaurant features tasty Mexican food and also distributes fresh tortillas throughout the Central Coast. Its amazing tortilla machine churns out something like 14,000 dozen tortillas a day!

You'll soon reach Milpas Street, the main thoroughfare of the Hispanic neighborhood. It's the center of the community, a place where you'll hear more Spanish than English. It's home to thousands of Santa Barbarans, some of whom are recent immigrants, others who can trace their roots back to the very beginnings of Santa Barbara.

If you're hungry, head up Milpas Street a few blocks to the corner of Alphonse for one of Santa Barbara's most renowned restaurants, La Super-Rica. Julia Child has been quoted saying it's her favorite Mexican restaurant.

Directions: Begin this walk at State and Haley. The Downtown/Waterfront Shuttle takes to you the corner of State and Haley. If you walk the length of Haley to Milpas, you can bus back to State Street via Gutierrez Street, one block south.

Elings Park
Sierra Club Trail

1-mile loop; to Jesuit Hill is 1.5 miles round trip

Elings Park has everything a park should have: a developed side with picnic tables, soccer and softball fields, a BMX track, a war memorial and an amphitheater; also a wild side with vista points and hiking trails. Some park professionals call it "a model park for the future."

Such acclaim comes not so much from its amenities (which are considerable) but from its style of operation: the park is a private one, open to the public, but operated without governmental assistance by a private foundation. Formerly known as Las Positas Friendship Park, it was renamed Elings Park in 1999 in recognition of the considerable financial contribution to the park's support by Dr. Virgil Elings and his family.

Because no tax dollars go to the support the park, efforts to gain sponsorship/funding for park facilities are extraordinary; some of these efforts may bring a smile to some park visitors. Everything appears to be sponsored, from the Wells Fargo Amphitheater to a massive oak tree, "To provide shade for all of Santa Barbara," courtesy of Mercedes-Benz. Traffic circle landscaping, picnic sites and even a flagpole are similarly sponsored. Certainly the site has come a long way since its use as a city dump.

All of these park partnerships and north side improvements are more or less academic to hikers who trek the wild, south side of the park. Thus far, the park foundation has left well enough alone.

Recently the park more than doubled in size when 136 adjoining acres long known as the Jesuit Property was acquired. The California Province of the Society of Jesus (the Jesuits) purchased the property back in 1927 with the intention of building a seminary to train men for the priesthood.

Certainly the then-isolated site with its mountain and ocean views might have been an ideal place for contemplation and the spiritual life. However, the number of men entering the priesthood declined and the seminary was never built. The land was offered for sale several times to developers with plans to build a resort, an up-scale retirement home, and even a performing arts center, but a deal was never finalized.

Sierra Club Trail, constructed by the local chapter's volunteers, loops up and along a north-facing ridge high above the developed part of the park. From the ridgetop, the walker gets an unusual view of downtown

Santa Barbara, as well as its Riviera and Santa Ynez Mountains backdrop. You can walk from the ridgetop over to Jesuit Hill, a 500-foot wide promontory and hang-glider launch offering grand view of the coast and Channel Islands.

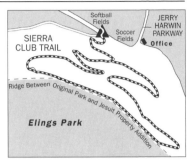

Directions: From Highway 101 in Santa Barbara, exit on Las Positas Road and drive a mile south (toward the coast) to the entrance for Elings Park on the left. Follow the park road (Jerry Harwin Parkway) to the signed trailhead on the right and to plenty of roadside parking.

The Walk: Sierra Club Trail begins a mellow ascent through a tunnel of fennel. The licorice-scented thickets are joined by oak, some poison oak (careful), sage and various members of the coastal scrub community.

Just as the trail crests the ridge it bends sharply east and immediately gains a viewpoint. Park yourself on a boulder or the stonewall of the vista and admire the municipal view.

Continue along the ridgetop route. Sierra Club Trail makes a hairpin turn and starts its descent back to the trailhead, but if you'd like to extend your walk, follow the less obvious trail skirting the agricultural fields and leading to the top of wide flat—Jesuit Hill. Colorful streamers fluttering above the fennel tell hang-gliders wind direction.

When you walk Jesuit Hill you can understand why this land resisted developers; it's a very steep slope and sparsely vegetated, with brick-hard clay soil. If you choose, you may walk one of the two dirt roads that extend from the top of the hill down toward a locked gate entry on Cliff Drive.

Enjoy the coastal and mountain views, then retrace your steps back to the Sierra Club Trail for the short descent back to the trailhead.

Veterans Memorial Walk, Terrace of Remembrance

THIS CONTEMPLATIVE WALK is simultaneously a somber reminder of those individuals who made the ultimate sacrifice for their country—and a celebration of the best of American life. The view of grassy ball fields where children skip and play, where families throw Frisbees and toddlers climb onto colorful playground equipment may sound incongruous, but there's poignancy in viewing so much life amidst so much loss of life.

California poppies and sweet alyssum add color and fragrance to the hillside which is also planted with 98 incense cedar trees, positioned as sentinels standing guard, one for each of Santa Barbara's fallen during the Vietnam War.

Continue along the path, pausing at each bougainvillea-topped marker engraved with the names of those who died in each year of the long and terrible war. Stop at the Terrace of Remembrance plaza to admire the graceful

The Terrace of Remembrance with its sad tableaux.

globe and reflect on the names of each of Santa Barbara County's war dead since the state of California entered the Union on September 9, 1850. You'll notice the names of at least one woman, several prominent families, many ethnicities, and, sadly, that there is room on one tablet for future use. We can only hope it will remain empty for years to come.

Follow the stair-step path up the hill, pausing at the oak-shaded picnic grounds for quiet contemplation before returning to the parking lot where an American flag flies proudly in the breeze. Stop for another moment to admire the expansive view of Santa Barbara.

Directions: Enter Elings Park and drive past BMX track and ball fields to the end of the road where the sign reads Godric Grove/Singleton Day Camp. Turn left and follow the narrow, winding road a short way to the parking lot. You'll pass the trailhead with its handsome sandstone entrance on your left. Return on foot to the trailhead and follow the path along the hillside.

Only on Sunday

1 mile or so for the Art Show

On Sundays in Santa Barbara, Cabrillo Boulevard is transformed into a colorful art and craft show. The Cabrillo Art & Craft Show extends one-half mile along Cabrillo Boulevard from Stearns Wharf. So figure a mile round trip.

Directions: The Cabrillo Boulevard exit from Highway 101 brings you to the art walk, and to Stearns Wharf. By midday, nearby parking might be difficult to find.

MTD: Downtown/Waterfront Shuttle to Stearns Wharf.

The Walk: Starting at Stearns Wharf, and extending eastward for about a half-mile along palm-lined Chase Palm Park, is one of Santa Barbara's must-see attractions. Every Sunday, Cabrillo Boulevard is transformed into a colorful bazaar featuring the work of the most talented local artists and artisans. Hand-crafted clothing, jewelry and leather goods, pottery and ceramics, paintings and baskets, wind chimes and whimsical items that defy categorization are for sale; many of the artists are on hand to discuss their work with you. There is some truly fine artwork—especially paintings and photographs—to be found on the walk, and many more crafts. Enjoy the show and the view.

When you've seen all the arts and crafts you can handle (or when you've run out of money paying for the ones you want to take home with you), return to Stearns Wharf

Celebrate Sundays with arts, crafts, and plenty of fun.

Santa Barbara Cemetery

1 mile around the grounds

View some notable frescoes, see a classic building designed by Santa Barbara's best-known architect, and stroll the quiet grounds that have served as the community's final resting place for more than a century. Don't expect grandiose Forest Lawn-like attractions, but there's a wonderful chapel here designed by famed architect George Washington Smith.

Cemeteries seem to inspire stories and Santa Barbara's is no exception. Aldous Huxley is said to be buried in an unmarked grave somewhere on the property. And local lore has it that several barons, princes, dukes and counts—who never even visited Santa Barbara—are buried here because it's known as one of the most beautiful cemeteries in the world.

Some think cemeteries are peaceful places that provide a glimpse into the culture, values and people of a place. Others find them depressing, even morbid. If you fall into the latter category, skip this walk. But if you fall into the former, come along with us.

Directions: Exit Highway 101 on Cabrillo Boulevard (a left-lane off-ramp). Turn oceanward on Cabrillo and be prepared to make an awkward left turn (be very careful) on Channel Drive. Look sharply right for the drive leading to the cemetery.

The Santa Barbara Cemetery is located at the east end of Cabrillo Boulevard, where it meets Channel Drive (a road that used to go up to the Biltmore Hotel; storm damage wiped out one lane near the hotel so the motorist can only descend Channel Drive from the Biltmore). Park near the Sanctuary of Life Eternal.

MTD: Line 14 Montecito drops you off on the right, just past the cemetery entrance.

The Walk: Walk past the "Visitors Welcome" sign into the chapel, a fine place for contemplation before you begin your walk around the grounds. Designed in 1926 by architect George Washington Smith, the graceful Romanesque-Gothic chapel has long been regarded as one of his masterpieces.

Admire the murals, frescoes applied to the interior walls by famed Mexican painter Alfredo Ramos Martinez. After Smith's death in 1930, his widow commissioned Martinez to paint the frescoes. The striking artwork is a must-see for every art enthusiast.

Linger awhile to absorb the impact of the fine artwork with its garlands of flowers, handmaidens, monks and nuns moving toward the startlingly dominant figure of the resurrected Christ. Then wander

It's a heavenly view from the Santa Barbara Cemetery.

through the chapel, noting the markers of several notable Santa Barbarans. Architects George Washington Smith and Lutah Maria Riggs are both interred in the chapel wall. Downstairs from the chapel is a Gothic-style columbarium worth a look, and across the way is the Mausoleum in the Pines.

Uphill from the chapel is the cemetery's military section, marked with an American flag and a large cannon. Stroll through and you'll note that veterans from every war since the Civil War are buried here. From this hillock is a wonderful view—from the Santa Ynez Mountains to the Riviera and on to the ocean. It's nice to think that the permanent residents are enjoying the spot. At least their visitors do.

Head uphill and rightward toward the family mausoleum area. Notice tombs in styles representing everything from a classic Greek temple to an Egyptian pyramid. Read some of the headstones and markers; they tell many stories. Look for a brotherhood of young motorcyclists laid to rest in one section, infants and young children in another. Grouped in other sections are immigrants of Italian, Greek, Mexican, Chinese, Japanese and English ancestries.

At the southwest end of the cemetery, peer over the fence for a view of the magnificent Clark mansion. The 22-acre estate, "Bellosguardo" (beautiful lookout), was once the summer home of turn-of-the-20th-century U.S. Senator William A. Clark. Beyond the estate is a lovely view of the harbor.

Continue walking in a counter-clockwise circuit of the cemetery. On the oceanward side of the drive, on the bluffs, are buried many of Santa Barbara's one-time civic leaders including Pearl Chase, Thomas More Storke, and the Castagnola brothers. Continue east, then loop back toward the chapel, and look for the cemetery's oldest headstones that date back to the 19th century.

Montecito

From Montecito Village to Butterfly Beach is 1.5 miles or so round trip

Montecito has always been one of Santa Barbara's most fashionable neighborhoods. This easy walk takes you from a historic hotel, through a lovely shopping area to Butterfly Beach, the Biltmore and more. The Franciscan padres once considered Montecito for the site of their Mission, but decided against it because of the abundance of grizzly bears and wolves in the area. The lovely spot became a rich agricultural area in the nineteenth century, and a playground-hideaway for the rich and famous ever since. Although there are a few modest Montecito dwellings, in some neighborhoods the term "Montecito mansion" is redundant; the area is noted for its stately homes, quiet tree-lined streets and decidedly affluent ambience.

Old-time movie stars frequented the Montecito Inn, a Mediterranean-style hotel first owned by Hollywood's own Charlie Chaplin and "Fatty" Arbuckle. Located on the corner of Coast Village Road and Olive Mill Road, the hotel still maintains its original style and charm.

Directions: From Highway 101 at Olive Mill Road. Park on, or near, Coast Village Drive. This walk begins in front of the Montecito Inn, 1295 Coast Village Road.

MTD: Line 14 Montecito, with the bus stop at Coast Village Road and Hot Springs Road. Also Line 20, the Carpinteria connection.

The Walk: Head down the sidewalk past several excellent restaurants, interesting shops, and quite an assortment of real estate offices. Stop for a bite, browse a while and speculate—if your pocketbook allows. Enjoy the feeling and sophisticated elegance of the area, sometimes called the Rodeo Drive of Santa Barbara.

At Butterfly Lane, turn left and descend a stairwell into the pedestrian tunnel that takes you under the freeway. Stroll the estate-lined street to its end and head for the coastal accessway at Butterfly Beach.

Continue east along the beachfront road, Channel Drive, to Biltmore Beach and its Coral Casino, site of numerous glittering social events. The Coral Casino, with a restaurant and Olympic-size swimming pool, is a private beach club.

Admire the Biltmore, which has set the Santa Barbara standard for elegance since it opened in 1927. The gracious architecture and lovely grounds are something to behold.

Stay with Channel Drive as it turns inland and becomes Olive Mill Road, leading you over the freeway to Coast Village Road and your starting point.

Montecito's Upper Village

It's the ultimate picnic destination, a wonderful shopping excursion, and a delightful stroll down a country lane lined with storybook cottages. All this in less than a mile's walk.

Start at Montecito's Plaza del Sol, at the corner of San Ysidro and East Valley roads. Walk east on East Valley Road, facing traffic, for just two blocks. Turn left onto Periwinkle Lane and stroll amidst a wonderland of eucalyptus and oak trees, morning glory vines and lovely gingerbread houses. This fairytale neighborhood was built in the 1940s by architect Harriet Moody.

Follow Periwinkle Lane as it curves around to Hodges, turn left, then right on East Valley Road and return to your starting point. Explore the shops here and at Coast Village Road across the street, dine at the popular Italian eateries Piatti or Pane e Vino Trattoria.

For an unforgettable treat, don't miss Pierra LaFond and Company, an upscale gourmet foodstuffs/department store like no other. Here you may order deluxe treats for a sumptuous picnic. Then head south a few blocks down San Ysidro Road to Manning Park. Spread your luncheon and savor the day.

Directions: From Highway 101 in Montecito, exit on San Ysidro Road. Proceed north to the intersection with East Valley Road. Park at or near the shopping center.

MTD: Line 14 Montecito to East Valley Road and San Ysidro Road.

San Ysidro Creek Preserve
San Ysidro Creek Trail

From San Leandro Lane to East Valley Road is 2.5 miles round trip

Montecito, one of coastal California's priciest and most rustic residential areas, has a park that seems very much in keeping with its neighborhood. You half expect a gated entry or valet parking for San Ysidro Creek Preserve.

The Land Trust for Santa Barbara County secured 44 acres alongside San Ysidro Creek, a portion of the once sprawling estate of avid polo player Elmer Boeske. After the preserve was established in the late 1980s, some new paths have been constructed and signed by the Montecito Trails Foundation, but otherwise preserve stewards wisely decided to leave well enough alone.

A few miles of pathway explore oak woodland, and meander among rows of olive trees and eucalyptus. This is a preserve set aside for nature

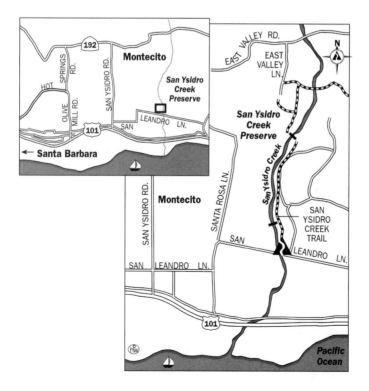

A creekside wilderness on San Ysidro Creek.

study and reflection rather than as a park for picnicking and playing; it's a good place for a quiet walk.

Directions: From Highway 101 in Montecito, exit on San Ysidro Road. Head briefly north and make a right on San Leandro Lane. Jog left on Hixon Road, then right again back onto San Leandro Lane, which you follow to a, pump-house, a white picket fence and San Ysidro Creek Preserve on the north side of the lane. Park carefully along the lane.

The Walk: From the white picket fence, wander among the great oaks for 100 yards and cross a handsome stone bridge over San Ysidro Creek. After a short half-mile, the path emerges from the trees and joins paved Ennisbrook for 100 yards. The trail resumes and drops back to the creek.

After a bit more woodsy walking, you'll cross another stone bridge over San Ysidro Creek and soon reach a junction. Take the left fork, which leads to a cul-de-sac at the end of East Valley Lane. Walk briefly north up the lane to a signed junction with a footpath leading east. (Those walkers wishing to visit Montecito's Upper Village, can continue up the lane to it junction with East Valley Road. Turn left [west] and walk 0.5 mile along the road to the village and its shops and restaurants. The road is busier than you'd expect and there's not too much shoulder to walk in places, so be careful.)

Travel among the oaks to another junction. If you proceed straight the path soon crosses San Ysidro Creek, then winds through a eucalyptus forest before it dead-ends a short distance later. The right fork heads south and you'll soon be retracing your steps back to the trailhead.

Great Gates of Montecito

"GOOD FENCES make good neighbors," wrote Robert Frost, but he never mentioned gates. If he had traveled west, however, no doubt he would have found sheer poetry in the impressive wrought-iron portals that guard the great estates of Montecito.

There are two sides to every gate, but many ways to view them: Gates provide those who live beyond them with a measure of privacy, protection and—let's face it—prestige. They serve as a screen between the street and the grounds, separating the lives of the rich and privileged from the prying eyes of the curious. They bid welcome to invited guests and impose a formidable barrier to the outsider.

But looking at the gate, rather than beyond it, becomes an exercise in viewing art, the gallery for which is the quiet country lanes of Montecito.

Forged from steel and worked by hand, the intricate, ornately filigreed designs exemplify the craftsmanship and artistry of a great Santa Barbara tradition. Several ornamental ironworkers carry on today, mindful of the standards set by great masters such as Walter Cordero, Gunnar Thiest and E.J. Craviotto.

A generation ago, all parts of a wrought-iron gate, including ornamental flowers, birds, finials and handrails, were pounded out of hot iron, a single piece at a time. Today, the decorative prefabricated components are largely mass-produced, at considerable savings in time and money.

Take a rambling Sunday drive along Sycamore Canyon Road, Cold Spring Road, East Mountain Drive, Hot Springs Road, East Valley Road and Park Lane.

The gates of Lotusland—the fabulous garden now open to the public on a limited basis—were fashioned in 1946 by E.J. Craviotto, who drew the design on the floor of his shop and charged Ganna Walska $1,200 for his work.

Estimated cost today? Tens of thousands of dollars for a simple, airy set of gates designed to be seen, admired and opened by invitation only (today by reservation).

Lotusland

0.5 mile stroll (garden open by reservation only)

Behind the cactus-bordered pink stucco walls and iron gates in the heart of Montecito lies one of the great gardens of the world. Perhaps most enchanting are the one-hundred year old lotus ponds that gave this land its name. And Lotusland is much more—a bamboo forest, a fantasyland of aloes, oversized Japanese gardens and an eclectic Eden of rare trees and shrubs from around the world.

Lotusland is every bit as whimsical and welcoming, beautiful and eccentric as its creator—opera star and arts patron Madame Ganna Walska.

Madame came from Poland, where she was born in 1884. At 17 she married Baron Arcadie D'Eingorne—the first of a series of wealthy husbands. Her beauty and beautiful voice attracted the attention of Russian high society and soon she was hobnobbing with the czar and his court.

She began her opera career in Europe and traveled to America where she adopted her stage name of Walska, which means waltz in her native Polish. Reviews of the diva's performance were decidedly mixed, but her career was certainly boosted by the millions spent by her fourth husband, Harold McCormick, chairman of International Harvester.

Madame Walska bought the famed Thèatré des Champs-Élysses in Paris. She entertained lavishly in her château near Versailles, sang with Caruso in New York, and created a sensation wherever she traveled on two continents. Madame also embarked on a path of self-discovery. She practiced yoga, meditated with Meher Baba, and consulted palmists, psychoanalysts, and the ouija board.

About 1940, although she had never visited the West Coast, California began calling her. "Intuitively, I knew the day would come when I would go to that Golden State," she wrote in her 1941 autobiography, *Always Room at the Top*. "I felt positive that one time or another I should live there . . . perhaps even finish my earthly existence there. . . ."

Madame Ganna Walska settled in Montecito in 1941. She bought a Montecito estate and began fashioning her extensive gardens. Working close to the earth seemed to ground her and she soon dumped her sixth and last husband, Theos Bernard, self-styled yogi and White Llama. After Bernard's departure, she changed the name of her state from Tibetland to Lotusland.

The passion that Madame brought to the arts in New York, Chicago, London and Paris, she now channeled into her garden. And the garden grew with collections of palms, groves of rare citrus, and even a Chinese deciduous redwood that for many years was thought to be the last living representative of an all-but-extinct species.

Madame consulted the leading architects of the day, but she herself made the major decisions of what was planted where in Lotusland. To be sure, some of her creations can only be called eccentric. One corner of the garden, called "The Pond," defies description. Imagine Mono Lake pumped all-but-dry. Then add an abalone-shell shoreline and waterfalls cascading over giant clams.

There's a whimsical topiary menagerie in the shapes of dogs, rabbits, donkeys and bears. And suspended over the swimming pool is one

of Madame's favorite works of art—a 1957 Chevy hood sculpted into a pelican.

Drought-tolerant shrubs and cacti from five continents are planted in abstract patterns. The effect is beautiful, but bizarre. Depending on the light and the garden-goer's mood, the weird whorls of succulents seem a creation of either Gustave Doré or Jackson Pollack.

Lotusland holds one of the world's most extensive collections of cycads, tropical shrubs and trees resembling thick-stemmed palms, hung with huge cones that contain fleshy seeds. Cycads evolved more than 200 million years ago, well before the appearance of flowering plants on earth. It's easy to imagine dinosaurs munching the leathery, fern-like leaves.

Madame Walska loved mass plantings of the same color and one of the garden's most stunning sights is a sweeping, other-worldly cluster of blue cycads, a corner of Lotusland where the earth collides with the sky.

When Madame died in 1984, she was 100 years old and had spent most of the last four decades of her life working in her garden. One reason she worked so hard is because she believed in reincarnation, and thought that the more she got done in this life, the less she would have to do in the next.

Lotusland is open to visitors by appointment only. Call the Lotusland Foundation for reservations: (805) 969-9990.

Old Town Goleta

0.75 mile round trip

Step into the past and contemplate the future with a stroll along Hollister Avenue, the one-time heart of old Goleta, and its "Main Street" today. After several elections, what was once the largest unincorporated area in California finally became a city in November 2001. While the economic heart of the new city lies elsewhere, the visitor will discover a certain sentimental appeal in the area known as Old Town.

Goleta (Spanish for "small ship" or "schooner") was once known for its fertile farmland and its high-quality citrus orchards. (Even today, the annual Goleta Lemon Festival is a popular event.)

In 1956, the Studebaker-Packard Corporation became the first aerospace company to move to Goleta when it established a research and development facility on Hollister Avenue. For Goleta, it's been high-tech ever since. The establishment of the University of California at Santa Barbara and an expansion of the nearby airport also contributed to the Goleta Valley's rapid transformation from prosperous farming region to a technology research center and suburban bedroom community.

Old Town Goleta is a mix of old and new, where reminders of times gone by are obviously in line for renovation. Those who dream big will find lots of potential here; many already have. Old Town's inspiring mix of small, mom-and-pop businesses, many established by immigrant families, offer evidence that the American Dream lives in small towns—and in brand-new cities.

Directions: From Highway 101 in Santa Barbara, take Clarence Ward Memorial Boulevard (217) and almost immediately exit onto Hollister Avenue. Turn right (west) and drive a few blocks to the Goleta Valley Community Center (5679 Hollister) located on the south side of the avenue. Park along Hollister or at the community center.

Another way to go: From Highway 101 in Goleta, exit on Fairview Avenue and head briefly south to Hollister Avenue. Turn left and drive a few blocks to the Goleta Valley Community Center.

MTD: The restored historic bus stop in front of the Goleta Valley Community Center gets lots of use with several MTD routes coming and going here, including Line 6 State/Hollister Traveler, Line 11 Downtown/UCSB Connection, Line 12 UCSB/Goleta Express.

The Walk: Stroll around Goleta Valley Community Center, a handsome Spanish Revival-style building constructed as the Goleta Union School in the 1920s. The center hosts the Boys and Girls clubs, as well as many community programs.

A bit of the old, anticipation of the new on Goleta's main street.

In front of the center, note the graceful gazebo, dolphin sculpture, a stone with a historic plaque commemorating the De Anza expedition and the El Camino Real mission bell. Imagine the sandal-clad Spanish padres walking the dusty Mission Trail as you walk west on Hollister past 1950s-style stucco buildings housing businesses that are mostly dedicated to the care of the car.

Follow your nose to The Habit, a funky hamburger stand; the chili-cheese fries are a great post-walk snack. Pause at the corner of Hollister and Rutherford to read the historic marker that explains the origins of a building formerly known as Ovington's Hangar. After serving as a show-room for tractors and other farm equipment, the cavernous structure became a market in 1955. Santa Cruz Market is the kind of place where you can buy a colorful piñata, pumpkin candy, pan dulce, or even a tor-tilla press.

Walk past the incongruity of an ATM positioned next to a blacksmith shop. A longtime Italian restaurant, where the owner sang opera as he served steaming plates of pasta, is now Oriental Market and Seafood. Peruse the Malaysian cake, fortune cookies, exotic canned goods and spices, and admire the uniquely shaped lucky bamboo plants.

At the intersection of Fairview and Hollister, look for the home of a palm reader who offers advice on all matters: love, marriage, business, past, present, future. Look for the graceful mural tucked behind the Jiffy Lube, and celebrate the triumphant beauty of earth and renewal. Cross the busy intersection with the light to the other side of Hollister. Ignore the mission-inspired architecture of a national taco chain, and turn your attention instead to three shops with unique façades. In the early days of the 20th century, O.D. Coffey's Grocery stood at 5968; with its popular soda fountain and well-stocked shelves, it was a vital part of the community. At the same time, a blacksmith shop occupied the building at 5960. At 5892, pause to admire the Spanish Colonial Revival structure built in 1934; formerly a post office, bank and law office, today it houses a popular—and very healthy restaurant—The Natural Café.

Continue to the corner of Magnolia, and take a look at the Craftsman-inspired apartment building at 170 Magnolia. Originally built as a hotel in 1915, it's one historic structure left on a street of apartment buildings that have seen better days.

Walk along Hollister once more and admire the fine old tilework that is evidence of earlier efforts to spruce up the street. Stroll past a mix of commercial establishments to the corner of Nectarine and a group of tiny, light-blue rental cottages, once part of the Carmel Motor Court.

Between Nectarine and Tecolote on Hollister is Goleta's Old Town Mall, featuring a curious arcade, several colorful awnings, and an unusually elevated strip of sidewalk. Note the offices of the *Valley Voice*, the community, er, city newspaper that serves as the voice of the Goleta Valley. The free paper is distributed every Friday and is a good source of information for the area.

At 5744, current home of a Japanese restaurant, examine the faded lettering on the wall: the site formerly housed Justice Court and the offices of the local constable and justice of the peace. Continue to the Goleta Professional Building, home to an assortment of small business, ranging from CPAs to a driving school and several computer companies. Imagine how this spot could be—and no doubt will be—refurbished and spruced up into an attractively appointed office park.

Press the crosswalk button for a high-tech solution to a pedestrian problem. At a location that was once perilous crossing for those on foot, the button activates a recorded message, as well as lights on the street surface to warn oncoming vehicles to stop. (Trust your instincts anyway, and be very careful crossing this busy street.) Return to the start—or do a little shopping and snacking—and contemplate the possibilities that await Goleta, California's newest city.

Lake Los Carneros County Park
Los Carneros Trail
1-mile loop around lake

Airline passengers on take-off and approach to the Santa Barbara Municipal Airport are often surprised at how rural the Goleta Valley still appears. Despite decades of development, the valley, from the air anyway, looks green with orchards, a rural enclave tucked between the Santa Ynez Mountains and the sea.

Goleta Valley, as viewed from the ground often presents a less bucolic face: subdivisions, shopping centers and industrial parks. Still, a rural valley remains and you can get a good glimpse of it at Lake Los Carneros County Park, which harbors many reminders of Goleta days gone by.

Railroad buffs are attracted to the Goleta Depot, built in 1901 and moved in 1981 to the park. An historic freight office, passenger waiting area and a caboose are some of the highlights. Another attraction is an excellent model railroad exhibit that uses the Santa Barbara-Goleta area of yesteryear as a backdrop. On weekend afternoons, a miniature train offers rides around the depot.

Across from the railroad depot is Stow House, a two-story Victorian built by Goleta pioneer Sherman P. Stow in 1872. The restored house, furnished with antiques of the era, is open for touring on the weekends.

Outside the house is an old gravity-fed gas pump and a hand-cranked water pump. An old red barn and the barnyard houses the Horace Sexton Memorial Museum of farm implements and machinery.

Enjoy Stow House's Victorian design and elegant furnishings.

Enjoy a saunter along the shore, but please don't feed the fowl.

Finally, for hikers and birdwatchers, the park has a trail circling Lake Carneros, once part of the irrigation system for the Stow family's citrus orchards. Now the little lake is patrolled by a flotilla of water birds, including mallard, canvasback, teal, geese and egrets.

Another natural highlight is the wintering population of monarch butterflies, which cluster in great numbers in the park's eucalyptus grove.

Directions: From Highway 101 in Goleta, exit on Los Carneros Road and turn north (toward the mountains). Drive a quarter mile to Lake Los Carneros County Park on the right. Parking is free.

MTD: Line 10 Cathedral Oaks with the stop at Cathedral Oaks and Los Carneros.

The Walk: Stroll past Stow House and the yard full of farming implements toward the lake. A wide path bears right, but you look left for a steeper, narrower trail that descends briefly, but steeply down to Lake Los Carneros. A long wooden footbridge offers duck- and turtle-watching opportunities, as well as passage to the other side.

The path then skirts the park's monarch butterfly-hosting eucalyptus grove before emerging on an open area above the lake. When the path reaches the dam on the lake's south side, you may choose to walk right by the lakeshore or atop an embankment. From up top, you get a view of the two Goletas: To the south is the surprisingly busy airport, the University of California at Santa Barbara, the freeway, and the industrial sector. To the north lies the lake, neatly terraced orchards and the bold, unperturbed beauty of the Santa Ynez Mountains.

To complete your clockwise circuit of Lake Los Carneros, continue following the path along the west side of the lake back to the Goleta Depot and the parking area.

University of California at Santa Barbara

1 mile round trip

UCSB is the third-largest UC campus. Although the university has a "party school" reputation, it's also known for excellent academic programs. While the campus architecture is, to say the least, uninspired, the stunning coastal location makes up for the dull buildings. And you have to see Isla Vista, with its remarkably high student population.

The University of California at Santa Barbara was thrust into the national spotlight during the 1960s when war protestors burned the Isla Vista Bank of America. Today, everything is comparatively peaceful, considering that the community is one of the most densely populated in all of California. Adjacent to campus are high-rise student-housing buildings, fraternity rows and sorority houses. Bike paths crisscross the campus, indeed the entire Isla Vista area, and they receive heavy use. When walking through the area, be sure to use caution when crossing bike paths

Directions: The isolated campus is actually located in Isla Vista, 10 miles from downtown Santa Barbara.

If you're arriving by car, take Highway 101 to Goleta, veering south on Clarence Ward Memorial Boulevard (217) and following the signs to UCSB. At the entry kiosk on weekdays, you'll pay a parking fee and receive a campus map and directions. There's convenient parking in a lot off University Road opposite North Hall.

MTD: Line 9 Stow Canyon/UCSB Connection and Line 11 Downtown/UCSB Connection lead to the university campus.

The Walk: To explore the UCSB campus, start at Cheadle Hall, the university's administration building, which includes Admissions, Graduate Division, and the chancellor's office.

Head toward Campbell Hall, where films, lectures, dance, musical and theatrical performances are often featured. Take the diagonal pathway and head for the back entrance of the library, which houses nearly two million volumes. Inside the library, take the elevator up to the eighth floor for a wonderful view of the area. From the north windows, get a great view of the rugged Santa Ynez Mountains, with the airport on the right.

From the east windows, take in the view of Goleta Pier, and a surprising amount of open space. From this vantage point, it is obvious that Santa Barbara is some 10 miles downcoast from Isla Vista.

Give 'em a break: Students can't study all the time!

From the south windows, view dormitory housing across the way, the ocean and Channel Islands beyond. There are several favorite surfing, skin-diving, snorkeling and sun-worshipping beach spots nearby, including Campus Point, Depression and Sands.

Return to the first floor, and leave the library by the front door, heading west toward 175-foot Storke Tower, tallest structure in Santa Barbara County. The bell tower's observation deck is occasionally open. The bells chime at 10 minutes to the hour (class dismissed!) and on the hour (time for class to begin). The university's communication center is located at the base of the tower; the newspaper, yearbook and programs for public radio station KCSB-FM are produced here.

Adjacent to the tower is Storke Plaza, the usually bustling main quad area. Head toward University Center, called UCen by students. Inside are commercial services, including a travel agency, post office, copy center and typing service, along with three restaurants, the bookstore, a grocery store and entertainment room. The activities board just inside the hallway always offers plenty to do.

Head for the art museum which features exhibitions year-round, then stroll into Isla Vista, about five minutes away. It's a land of jumbo burgers, grande burritos and monster beers, falafel, coffee in every form, and pizza, pizza, pizza.

Solvang

From Mission Santa Ynez through downtown is 0.75 mile round trip

The small Danish-themed community of Solvang extends a hearty *velkom-men* to more than a million visitors a year. Many travelers are absolutely charmed by what seems to be a scene out of a Hans Christian Anderson story, while some visitors think the Bit o' Denmark theme is a bit over the top. Solvang is a walker-friendly town that offers numerous benches for resting. Conveniently located Solvang Park is an inviting locale for a pic-nic, and a good place for children to expend some of their pent-up energy.

The first Danish settlers came in 1911 and called this portion of the Santa Ynez Valley *Solvang* (sunny fields). Successive generations of Danish-Americans have worked hard to create authentic-looking build-ings and maintain an Old World atmosphere.

Danish architectural elements include half-timbered walls, thatched roofs and stained glass, as well as the extensive use of tile and copper. Walkers will enjoy strolling over cobblestone sidewalks and across cobbled courtyards.

Mission Santa Ynez, the 19th of California's 21 missions, borders Solvang on the east. Founded in 1804, the Mission was badly damaged in the great earthquake of 1812 and rebuilt a few years later. The Mission church has been in continuous use since 1817.

The Mission museum features artifacts from the Chumash, Spanish, Mexican and early American eras. Particularly intriguing are the European and Native American artwork—paintings, wood carvings and silverwork—and vestments worn by Padre Junípero Serra.

Don't miss a meditative stroll through the Mission garden, located in a quadrangle surrounded by Mission walls. The garden includes a hedge sculpted in the shape of a Celtic cross and some lovely old pepper trees.

Solvang boasts an intriguing history, a lively summer theater festival and an excellent strategic location in the midst of the Santa Ynez Valley wine country, but will likely continue to be best known as a place to shop. The village is chock-full of shops selling clothing, collectibles, dolls, knives, quilts, toys and much more.

Savor the fragrance of fresh Danish pastries that wafts from numer-ous bakeries, which display their treats in storefront windows located irresistibly close to passersby. For some walkers, a Solvang walk is a quest for the perfect *aebleskiver,* those Danish pancake balls, served with jam (usually raspberry) and powdered sugar.

Directions: Solvang is located some 45 miles upcoast and inland from Santa Barbara. Take Highway 154 past Cachuma Lake to Highway

Shoppe 'til you drop in scenic Solvang.

246, then head west into town. Or from Highway 101 in Buellton, exit on Highway 246 and follow it east into Solvang.

Park in the large lot at Mission Santa Ynez, located off Highway 246 or turn south off of 246 onto Alisal Road and drive a half block into town, where you'll spot Solvang's major parking lot.

The Walk: Stroll under the arches of the Mission and follow the arcade to its end. Join the asphalt pathway or the asphalt roadway and walk across the mission grounds to Alisal Street.

From Alisal, step into a courtyard to view the Round Tower, a one-third size replica of the Round Tower of Copenhagen. The original, completed in 1642, is Europe's oldest functioning observatory; Solvang's version was constructed in 1991.

Head west on Copenhagen Drive, the town's main shopping street. The 1600 block of Copenhagen Drive, features many 1920s buildings built by Solvang's original settlers.

Stop in at the Solvang Conference and Visitors Bureau information office. There's usually a well-informed person in Danish costume behind the desk eager to provide details about Solvang and the Santa Ynez Valley.

Walk over to 1680 Mission Drive (Highway 246), then upstairs from The Book Loft; here you'll find the Hans Christian Anderson Museum, which displays an impressive collection of memorabilia celebrating the life of the famous Danish storyteller.

For a deeper study of the area's Danish heritage, detour south on Second Street for a few blocks to Elverhoy Way and the Elverhoy Museum of Danish Heritage and Solvang History.

Hans Christian Anderson Park

1.3 miles round trip

Just a hop, skip and a jump from the pancake restaurants and pastry shops of Solvang is Hans Christian Anderson Park, where a hiking trail offers the chance to walk off those aebleskivers.

The park is only a quarter mile from "Little Denmark," but a world apart. True to its namesake author, it's a fairy tale setting of rolling green hills and antiquarian oaks. Adobe Creek meanders through the kid-sized (52-acre) bucolic preserve.

To say the park shares Solvang's Denmark-to-the-max theme, might be understatement. An impressive entry arch, built by the Danish Brotherhood Lodge, is supported by two towers of Danish design. One looks like a Danish church, the other resembles a castle tower, perhaps the one where Rapunzel let down her hair. The influence extends to an outdoor amphitheater, modeled after one in the mother country, and even to the heavy timbered restrooms and trashcans.

Directions: To get to Solvang, exit Highway 101 in Buellton and drive three miles east on Highway 246. From downtown Solvang, turn north on Atterdag Road, which turns into Chalk Hill Road in 0.3 mile. Almost immediately thereafter, turn left into Hans Christian Anderson Park. The park road leads under the entry arch and down to the canyon floor, where there's ample parking. Look for the signed Horse-Hiking Trail on the south side of the entry road.

The Walk: The park's path heads west down a semi-wild corridor between the edge of suburban Solvang to the south and the park's northside picnic grounds and tennis courts. En route are some truly enchanting oaks, with long mossy beards hanging from their branches.

The trail crosses Adobe Creek and dead-ends at Highway 246. For a change of scenery, join an alternate trail branching left from the main one; it leads back to the developed part of the park.

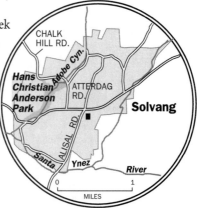

Coast

FROM CARPINTERIA west, the Santa Barbara County shoreline extends to Point Conception, one sandy and mellow beach after another. The coastline's southern exposure results in clearer water, smoother sand and warmer sun than other California communities. Or so the locals like to boast, anyway.

Awaiting the walker are miles of pleasant sand beach with the ocean and islands on one side and the mountains on the other. The beach is lined by a narrow coastal terrace that seems to protect it from residences, traffic, the hustle and bustle of the modern world.

Enhanced by the Mediterranean climate, Santa Barbara's beaches have long been world renowned for their beauty and a as a place to play. Sailing, surfing and sunbathing are popular shoreline activities.

Santa Barbara's coast has an ecological significance as well. Marine life is abundant and a large percentage of the state's fish and shellfish catch comes from the Santa Barbara Channel.

Many Santa Barbarans—and conservationists around the country—are concerned about the region's delicate ecology and fragile beauty. Oil drilling in the Santa Barbara Channel is particularly worrisome. The devastation brought by the 1969 oil spill is never far from the citizenry's mind. Debates about the offshore rigs and lease sales continue to this day.

For thousands of years before Europeans arrived, Chumash Indians, the most ocean-oriented of California's native peoples, lived along Santa Barbara's shores. They fished off the coast in dugout canoes, hunted in the nearby mountains. From the days of the missionaries and Spanish occupation through most of the nineteenth century, the coastline remained mostly undeveloped.

New England trading ships anchored offshore to take on a cargo of cowhides from local ranchers, but Santa Barbara was anything but a thriving seaport. Santa Barbara's "lighthouse" was a lantern hung at top of a tree known as "Sailors' Sycamore."

Lack of a safe port hindered Santa Barbara's development. The bay was merely a lovely curve in the coast, offering a landing place but no protection from the dreaded southeasters. Until John P. Stearns built his wharf in 1872, landing in Santa Barbara meant braving the breakers with small surfboats; passengers often got a bracing salt-water dip before arriving on shore.

With safe steamer landings, visitors—ranging from wealthy residents of colder climates looking for a place to winter to invalids (as they called them in Victorian times) seeking to restore their health—flocked to Santa Barbara. The "Sanitarium of the Pacific" got a big boost from Charles Nordhoff's 1872 bestseller *California for Travelers and Settlers,* which raved about Santa Barbara's charms and promoted it as a health resort.

Health-seekers and tourists gave Santa Barbara an international reputation, though world-class facilities to handle the visitors lagged far behind. Not until the Potter Hotel opened in 1902 was there a large oceanfront hotel. Fears of huge waves from Pacific storms meant the Arlington Hotel and others were built well inland.

For the entire twentieth century, the coastline was the subject of much debate among Santa Barbarans, between those who wanted to conserve the coast's natural beauty, and those who wanted to exploit the shore's full potential as a resort. Many Santa Barbarans wanted to ensure that only a wealthy tourist class came to Santa Barbara, while others welcomed out-of-town developers who built facilities to attract the middle class in great numbers. Both the Chamber of Commerce and wealthy philanthropists helped purchase oceanfront land and thwart tawdry developments and "undesirable amusements."

It was the automobile and a changing economy that brought changes to the waterfront. Wealthy part-time residents were not as influential as middle class auto tourists on vacation. After World War II came a motel boom that serviced these visitors.

Whether it's a large hotel project or the design of a small fountain, Santa Barbarans are likely to debate the issues of aesthetics versus economics, open space versus commercial building well into the 21st century. For years Santa Barbarans have debated the merits of a massive development proposed for the foot of State Street.

In addition to the picture postcard beaches near Santa Barbara, the county has another coast, a wild coast. The Gaviota Coast is a beautiful montage of mountains, bluffs and beaches. Local and national conservation groups are working to preserve this coast as national parkland in Gaviota National Seashore or, at the very least, see to it that it receives increased protection from development.

The county's north coast near Point Conception is characterized by rolling hills, marshlands and precipitous bluffs. A walk here is an unforgettable adventure. The county's northernmost coastline is dominated by the Guadalupe Dunes, the West Coast's highest dunes.

Rincon Point

From Rincon Point to Rincon Beach County Park is 0.5 mile round trip;
to Carpinteria State Beach is 6 miles round trip

The thirteen miles of coast extending between the Ventura River and Rincon Point is called "The Rincon," although it could be termed the Rincons, plural, because there are three indentations in the coast, separated by Pitas Point and Punta Gorda.

For surfers, the Rincon means Rincon Point, one of the best places to surf on the entire California coast. East of the point, surfers catch the swells refracted around the point and ride them near-parallel to shore. Some of Southern California's best waves break here in a foamy maelstrom, a true challenge for skilled kayakers and surfers.

For hikers, the cobble beaches downcoast from Rincon Point, are a challenge to walk. The ocean closely approaches Highway 101, especially at high tide when waves crash against the protecting rock embankment. For many years this stretch of coast was a barrier for travelers because one could pass only at low tide on the wet sands of the beach; at high tide, the waves dashed against the white cliffs of the mountains. Don Gaspar de Portolá on his way north in search of the Bay of Monterey, Father Junípero Serra as he traveled from mission to mission on foot, and John C. Frémont and his soldiers during the conquest of California all had to wait until the tide receded before they could pass.

In the early days of automobiling, a wooden plank causeway was built over the water. Columns of water occasionally shot through holes in the boards, startling horseless carriage drivers. Children shrieked in delight, though it proved distracting to their parents.

On the far side of Rincon Point is Santa Barbara County's Rincon Beach Park. In 1974, when beachgoers heard the park was slated to receive a heavy dose of cement paving and other "improvements," they staged a sit-in to protest. The powers that be were persuaded to pave less and preserve more. Today the park consists of a small picnic area, parking, and a coastal accessway.

This hike explores Rincon Point, made by the fan delta which built a sweeping spur into the ocean at the north end of Rincon Creek. The Santa Barbara–Ventura counties-dividing creek isn't long, but it descends precipitously from the hills and, at flood stage, carries boulders to the ocean. The longshore current can't move the large rocks, so they accumulate to make the rocky spur of the point. Consult a time table and walk only at low tide.

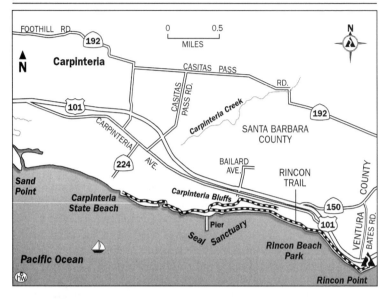

Directions: From Highway 101, about 12 miles upcoast from Ventura and 12 miles downcoast from Santa Barbara, exit on Bates Road. Head briefly south to the beach and the parking area for Rincon Point. You can also park in nearby Rincon Beach County Park if you choose.

The Walk: Walk down the coastal access-way between the busy freeway on your left and a line of eucalyptus on your right. Head upcoast over the cobble beach, passing a number of beachfront homes that are part of the residential community of Rincon.

Pause to watch the surfers work the point, then cross the mouth of Rincon Creek. Round Rincon Point on the cobblestone beach, pass a few more houses and the stairway up to Rincon Beach Park, and reach the sand strand.

Your beach-walk parallels the Southern Pacific railroad tracks, which are quite close the beach here. As you walk past the tiny community of Wave, you may ponder whether Wave was named for its proximity to the ocean or because people "waved" at the train going by.

High tide may necessitate a walk atop a seawall that borders a stretch of this beach. Two and a half miles of beach-walking brings you to the Chevron Oil Pier and Carpinteria State Beach.

Carpinteria Beach and Bluffs
Carpinteria Beach Trail

*From Carpinteria State Beach to Harbor Seal Preserve
is 2.5 miles round trip; to Carpinteria Bluffs is 4.5 miles round trip;
to Rincon Beach County Park is 6 miles round trip*

Carpinteria is one of the state park system's more popular beachfront campgrounds. A broad beach, gentle waves, fishing and clamming are among the reasons for this popularity. A tiny visitor center (open weekends only) offers displays of marine life and Chumash history, as well as a children-friendly tidepool tank.

Carpinteria residents boast they have "The World's Safest Beach" because, although the surf can be large, it breaks far out, and there's no undertow. As early as 1920, visitors reported "the Hawaiian diversion of surfboard riding." Surfers, hikers and bird-watchers have long enjoyed the bluffs, which rise about 100 feet above the beach and offer great views of Anacapa, Santa Cruz and Santa Rosa islands.

For more than two decades a battle raged between development interests with plans to build huge housing and hotel projects and local conservationists who wanted to preserve the bluffs, one of the last stretches of privately held, undeveloped coastline between Los Angeles and Santa Barbara.

Activists led by Citizens for the Carpinteria Bluffs and the Land Trust for Santa Barbara, along with local merchants, school children, hundreds of Santa Barbara county citizens and the California Coastal Conservancy raised money for the purchase of the property in 1998.

The Carpinteria tar pits once bubbled up near Carpinteria Beach. Spanish explorers noted that the Chumash caulked their canoes with the asphaltum. Long ago, the tar pits trapped mastodons, saber-toothed tigers and other prehistoric animals. Unfortunately, the pits, which may have yielded amazing fossils like those of the La Brea Tar Pits in Los Angeles, became a municipal dump.

On August 17, 1769, the Captain Portolá's Spanish explorers observed the native Chumash building a canoe and dubbed the location *la carpinteria,* the Spanish name for carpenter shop. The Chumash used the asphaltum to caulk their canoes and seal their cookware.

The Carpinteria beach hike heads downcoast along the state beach to City Bluffs Park and the Chevron Oil Pier. A small pocket beach contains the Harbor Seal Preserve. From December through May this beach is seals-only. Humans may watch the boisterous colony, sometimes numbering as many as 150 seals from a blufftop observation area above the beach.

After seal-watching, you can then sojourn over the Carpinteria bluffs or continue down the beach to Rincon Point on the Santa Barbara-Ventura county line.

Directions: From Highway 101 in Carpinteria, exit on Linden Avenue and head south (oceanward) 0.6 mile through town to the avenue's end at the beach. Park along Linden Avenue (free, but time restricted) or in the Carpinteria State Beach parking lot (fee).

MTD: Line 20 to Carpinteria Avenue and 7th Street. Walk 7th to Linden Avenue, and make a right. Continue to the beach.

The Walk: Follow "The World's Safest Beach" downcoast. After a half-mile's travel over the wide sand strand you'll reach beach-bisecting Carpinteria Creek. During the summer, a sand bar creates a lagoon at the mouth of the creek. Continue over the sand bar or, if Carpinteria Creek is high, retreat inland through the campground and use the bridge over the creek.

Picnic at City Bluffs Park or keep walking a short distance farther along the bluffs past Chevron Oil Pier to an excellent vista point above the Harbor Seal Preserve. From the seal preserve, you can walk another mile across the Carpinteria Bluffs. Time and tides permitting, you can continue still farther downcoast along the beach to Rincon Beach County Park, a popular surfing spot on the Santa Barbara-Ventura county line.

The hot Dog Man

NEAR THE SEAL PRESERVE are two more engaging destinations. The recently preserved Carpinteria Bluffs offer tranquil trails through eucalyptus groves and across open meadows.

If you like hot dogs, you'll love stopping at the All American Surf Dog, located on the Carpinteria Bluffs at the intersection of Highway 101 and the Bailard Avenue exit (the next exit up-coast from Bates Road, where this hike ends). Proprietor Bill Connell, a colorful character indeed, mans his mobile stand daily from 11 A.M. to 6 P.M. Or thereabouts.

You can't miss Connell's bright red cart, topped by a distinctive hot dog and a large American flag waving in the ever-present breeze. Customers, who range the gamut from hikers and surfers to businessmen and bus drivers, enjoy socializing while savoring the expansive open-air view of the mountains on one side and the ocean on the other.

Carpinteria Salt Marsh Nature Park

1 mile or so round trip

Carpinteria Salt Marsh is a remnant of a once far more vast wetland, several miles wide, that extended from the base of the Santa Ynez Mountains to the Pacific. Downtown Carpinteria stands on former marshland. A century of draining, filling and developing diminished the marsh to just 230 acres. Conservationists fought a 1960s-era yacht harbor/housing development (*à la* L.A.'s Marina del Rey) and condominium complexes proposed in the 1990s. Today the marsh is under the stewardship of the University of California reserve system.

Just a few years ago, the estuary was an eyesore, a wasteland of weeds and an unofficial dumpsite. After several years of restoration work that included removing tons of fill dirt and debris and planting thousands of native plants, the marsh has been greatly rehabilitated. When development was halted and limited water flow restored, the marsh helped healed itself.

The marsh is habitat for resident and migratory waterfowl as well as a nursery for halibut and other fish. Herons, egrets and the long-billed curlew are among the more commonly sighted birds in the reserve, where more than 200 species have been identified. Several endangered species, such as the salt marsh bird's beak, light-footed clapper rail and Beldings savannah sparrow survive at the marsh.

Directions: To reach Carpinteria Salt Marsh Nature Park, exit Highway 101 in Carpinteria on Linden Avenue. Just before road's end at Carpinteria City Beach, turn right (east) on Sandyland Road and drive three blocks to Ash Avenue at the entrance to the marsh. Park in the beach lot at the foot of Ash or along Ash Avenue itself.

The Walk: On the Ash Avenue side of the marsh, an amphitheater, restrooms, interpretive signs and access trails welcome the visitor. For a short mile's walk, meander north on the pathway that skirts the western edge of the wetland. Turn west alongside a mobile home park to the banks of Carpinteria Creek. Most estuary explorers will turn around here, though a pathway continues inland along the creek.

Summerland Beach
Summerland Beach Trail

*From Lookout County Park to Biltmore Beach
and Hotel is 5 miles round trip*

One might guess Summerland was named for the weather, but the name was taken from Spiritualist literature—something to do with the Second Heaven of Spiritualism. A century ago, Spiritualists pitched their tents on the tiny lots in Summerland.

The first offshore oil platform in the Western hemisphere was erected in Summerland's waters in 1896. Soon, more than three hundred wells were pumping oil from Pleistocene rocks at depths of 100 to 800 feet, an insignificant depth by today's standards.

Oil attracted far more people to Summerland than Spiritualism and soon the air was heavy with the smell of gas and oil. It was said illumination came easy—one simply pounded a pipe in the ground until reaching natural gas, and lit a match. Liberty Hall, the Spiritualists' community center, glowed with divine light and for a time Summerland became known as the "White City."

This walk travels due west along sandy Summerland Beach, rounds

Butterfly Beach: A favorite of locals and resort-goers for nearly a century.

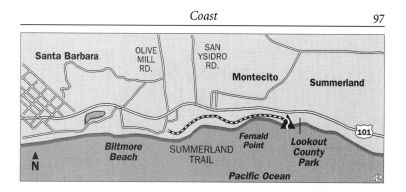

some rocky points, and concludes at the narrow beach in front of the famed Biltmore Hotel. Consult a tide table and walk only at low tide.

Directions: From Highway 101 in Summerland, take the Summerland exit and turn oceanward to Lookout County Park.

The Walk: Note the blufftop park's picnic area and a monument commemorating the first offshore oil rig, then descend a long asphalt ramp to the beach. From Lookout (Summerland) Beach, a sea wall extends 0.75 mile west to Fernald Point. At high tide, you may wish to walk atop it, but you might have to battle some brush. You soon pass a pretty little cove, bounded on the far side by Fernald Point, a fan delta deposited at the mouth of Romero Creek.

Rounding the point and approaching Montecito, observe the higher parts of the Santa Ynez Mountains on the northern skyline and the overturned beds of sandstone near the peaks. Montecito has no official public beaches, but most of the shoreline receives public use. Fernald–Sharks Cove is the first beach you travel, then Miramar Beach below the Miramar Hotel. Miramar-by-the-Sea was a popular watering place since the completion of the Southern Pacific Railroad line in 1901. The hotel, with its finely landscaped grounds and blue-roofed bungalows, used to be a passenger stop.

After a century of delighting seaside vacationers, the venerable hotel was sold to a New York billionaire, who partially razed the landmark and intends to construct a high-end resort. Delays in financing stalled the project and left local residents fuming at the eyesore.

In another 0.25 mile, hike across Montecito's third beach, Hammonds, popular with surfers. Hammonds Meadows on the bluffs above the beach is a former Chumash habitation and listed on the National Register of Historic Places. The bluffs were developed in the 1980s and '90s.

Upcoast from Hammonds you'll pass a number of fine homes and arrive at narrow Butterfly Beach, frequented by Biltmore Hotel guests as well as locals who enjoy the intimate, romantic setting. Opposite the beach is the magnificent Biltmore Hotel, built in 1927.

Stearns Wharf

0.5 mile or so round trip

Fun, fish and great sunset views are some of the highlights of a walk on the longest wharf between Los Angeles and San Francisco. It's not uncommon for the walker to overhear a half-dozen languages on the wharf; the most-visited Santa Barbara destination, it attracts visitors from around the world.

Before John Peck Stearns built his wharf in 1872, Santa Barbara, like so many California coastal towns, was isolated from the rest of the world. Only San Diego and San Francisco were blessed with natural harbors; other cities, big and small, needed some ingenuity to construct landing facilities.

Stearns provided the solution for Santa Barbara. With financial help from Colonel W.W. Hollister, the peg-legged lumber-yard owner built a long wharf—the longest, in fact, between Los Angeles and San Francisco. Passenger steamships could tie up at the 1,500-foot wharf, which greatly aided Santa Barbara's emergence as a health and vacation resort. Cargo ships unloaded the lumber and building materials so necessary for the city's Victorian-era building boom.

Steamships continued bringing thousands of visitors to Santa Barbara well into the 20th century, but as alternate means of transportation developed, the wharf's commercial importance began to decline. At the turn of the century, when the coastal rail line was finally completed, thus linking Santa Barbara to Los Angeles and San Francisco, many visitors began arriving by train. By the 1920s, a significant number of visitors arrived by automobile.

With more and more visitors, the wharf itself became a tourist attraction. The old yacht club building was converted to the Harbor Restaurant in 1941 and its reputation soon spread far and wide.

During World War II, the military took over Stearns Wharf and was less-than enthusiastic about its maintenance. Film star James Cagney and his brothers bought the wharf in 1945. The Cagney's ambitious plans for reconstruction never materialized when they realized that a small fortune in repairs was required.

Mario and George Castagnola purchased the wharf in 1955 and restored it. The Moby Dick Restaurant, gift shops, a bait-and-tackle shop and the Harbor Restaurant were popular with visitors during the 1950s and '60s. All of these structures were destroyed by fire in 1973.

The city took over the wharf's operation and, after several years of political and economic discussions, rebuilt it into the popular attraction it is today.

A fire burned the outer third of the wharf in a spectacular 1998 blaze. (A postcard of the wharf afire has proved more popular with tourists than the traditional view of the repaired wharf with the beautiful Pacific in the background. Hmmm . . .)

The wharf walk is one that just about everybody can—and should—do. Advice to heed comes in the form of two whimsical international signs posted at the foot of the wharf that read: "No high-heel shoes" and "No bare feet."

Directions: Stearns Wharf is located at the foot of State Street. Suggestion: Leave your car in one of the downtown parking lots and take the Downtown/Waterfront Shuttle to the wharf. Parking is limited on the wharf and the city encourages visitors to explore it on foot.

The Walk: At the beginning of the wharf, admire the dolphin fountain created by local artist Bud Bottoms. Copies of this fountain have been presented to Santa Barbara's sister cities.

If you read every plaque and interpretive panel on the wharf, you'll get quite an oceanography lesson. "Shifting Sands," "What Causes Tides?" and many more panels tell the story of Santa Barbara's islands, sea life and explorers.

The wharf offers great views of East Beach and Chase Palm Park, West Beach and the harbor. Don't forget to look inland toward downtown, the Riviera and the Santa Ynez Mountains. This view can also be enjoyed from the Harbor Restaurant and the outside deck of its bar.

Continue walking to the end of the wharf, perhaps ordering a shrimp cocktail to go. Cast a line and catch a fish of your own, as you'll notice many Santa Barbarans doing. A palm reader and a wine tasting room, as well as a few gift shops line the downcoast side of the wharf.

Visit the Nature Conservancy Visitor Center located out on the "dog leg" of the wharf. Exhibits highlighting the Conservancy's California preserves, as well as the organization's administrative offices are found here.

The Sea Center, currently undergoing restoration, presents some terrific exhibits of the marine life of Channel Islands National Park; it's a must-see, particularly for children-accompanied parents. This joint project with the Santa Barbara Museum of Natural History and the Channel Islands Marine Sanctuary features aquariums, an art gallery, a replica of a California gray whale and much more.

East Beach
East Beach Trail

From Stearns Wharf to Cabrillo Pavillion is 2.5 miles round trip; to Andree Clark Bird Refuge is 4 miles round trip

Historians credit architect Peter Barber with the idea for a palm-lined shoreline drive along East Beach. Barber got his idea after visiting tree-lined avenues in Europe. As mayor of Santa Barbara in 1891, he helped win voter approval for the bond measure that beautified the beach area and made Cabrillo Boulevard (then East Beach Boulevard) the scenic drive it is today.

Another visionary, perhaps the quintessential Santa Barbara citizen of her era, Pearl Chase, also crusaded to preserve the coastline. Chase and her brother Harold were honored when the city renamed Palm Park, created in 1931, Chase Palm Park.

The walker has three ways to explore East Beach: the sidewalk along Cabrillo Boulevard (the best option on Sundays when the weekly art sale takes place), along the beach itself, or (our favorite) a stroll through Chase Palm Park. The park is a bit more than a mile long. Near its east end is Cabrillo Pavillion, where you can break for refreshments, see an art show or rent a boogie board.

Directions: Begin at the foot of Stearns Wharf at the intersection of State Street and Cabrillo Boulevard. Park curbside on Cabrillo Boulevard (note the time restrictions) or in one of the fee lots on the beach side of Cabrillo.

MTD: Downtown/Waterfront shuttle down State Street to Stearns Wharf.

The Walk: Your path through *Washingtonia robusta* palms soon takes you over the mouth of Mission Creek.

At the foot of Santa Barbara Street, you'll find a plaque commemorating Pearl and Harold Chase for their civic and conservation efforts. You can't miss Skater's Point, a fabulous skateboard park constructed in 2000.

Cross Cabrillo Boulevard at Santa Barbara Street and step into the Chamber of Commerce Visitor Center, one of the tiniest buildings in town. Built in 1911, the sandstone structure formerly housed a fish market and restaurant. Maps and brochures are available at the center, open 9 A.M. to 5 P.M. Monday through Saturday; 10 A.M. to 4 P.M. on Sunday.

Cross Santa Barbara Street and enter an imaginatively landscaped length of Chase Palm Park. Pass a lovely courtyard and a fountain, then the historic merry-go-round. Admire the lovingly restored 1916 Allan Herchell carousel and cross a handsome bridge (created as an homage to the native Chumash) over a creek.

Meander a few more minutes beside a fanciful sand-play area bisected by a kid-size waterway to Shipwreck Playground. The playground, which has inspired many a "Titanic" re-enactment, features maritime-themed climbing structures and even whale sculptures that spout water. A high fence painted with a representation of the Santa Ynez Moutains shields park-goers from any glimpse of the city's least attractive side: railroad tracks, light industry, sewage treatment plant, and even a mothballed desalination plant.

After a bit more meandering through the palms you'll see Fess Parker's DoubleTree Resort on the north side of Cabrillo Boulevard. The large round building is a re-creation of a Southern Pacific Railway roundhouse, which was used to handle steam locomotives from 1926 to 1961.

The Mission Revival buildings take the historic Spanish motif and offer beach and mountain views. You can't miss the Chromatic Gate, the geometric rainbow situated on a corner across from the hotel.

Another Santa Barbara luxury hotel in Spanish style, located a little farther along Cabrillo Boulevard, is the Santa Barbara Radisson Hotel. Formerly the Vista Mar Monte, the hotel was completed in 1930 at a then-astronomical coast of $5 million, attracted film industry executives and Hollywood stars in the 1930s. During President Ronald Reagan's two terms in office, 1981-89, when Santa Barbara was the Western White House, the national press corps headquartered in the then-Sheraton.

A block inland from the Radisson Hotel is the Santa Barbara Zoological Gardens, a family-friendly zoo with more than 500 animals. At the end of Palm Park, skirt a small parking lot and proceed to Cabrillo Pavillion, where there's a café, as well as a bathhouse with changing rooms and beach equipment rentals.

Beyond Cabrillo Pavillion is another half-mile of East Beach with a turfed picnic area and very popular beach volleyballs courts. Those in the mood for beach-walking should head down to the shore; it's a bit more than a mile downcoast (passable at low tide) to the famed Biltmore Hotel and its narrow beach.

Otherwise, walk to the end of the picnic area and (carefully) cross Cabrillo Boulevard to Andree Clark Bird Refuge, where cormorants, egrets, herons and many species of ducks reside. Birdwatchers have sighted nearly 200 species in the 42-acre wildlife refuge.

The refuge was originally a tidal marsh, which some Santa Barbarans figured would make an ideal harbor. The Clark family donated monies to excavate the marsh and create a freshwater lake, which was named in memory of the donor's daughter, Andree.

You can follow the grass perimeter between the bike path and the lake shore about halfway around the lake. The path ends near a big bend in Cabrillo Boulevard.

Directly across the street from the end of the bike path is Las Aves, an office complex. Cross Los Patos Street and head into the courtyard area to view a colorful fountain entitled "It's Raining."

Il pleut, say the French, *stuhuy,* say the Chumash, *ame-ga butte imasu,* say the Japanese. Whatever the language, the whimsical fountain is a delight. Embedded with cracked pottery, cup handles, and bits of china; surely it's one-of-a-kind.

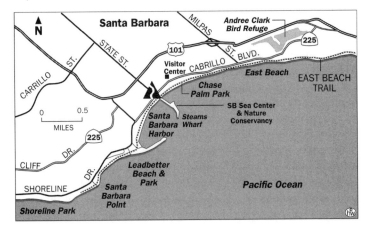

West Beach & Santa Barbara Harbor
West Beach Trail

Stearns Wharf to Harbor is 1.5 miles round trip;
to Shoreline Park is 3 miles round trip

Ever wonder where you could keep your 250-foot luxury yacht? No? Well, neither have we, but in the mid-1920s yeast magnate Max C. Fleischmann had quite a parking problem—no anchorage for his *Haida*. He donated $200 thousand to Santa Barbara to build a breakwater, if the city would match funds.

Unfortunately, city fathers and harbor boosters took Fleischmann up on his offer and ignored warnings of engineers who said a breakwater at West Beach would interrupt ocean currents and sand flow to beaches downcoast. The harbor was built at West Beach and almost immediately, downcoast beaches, from nearby Biltmore Beach to as far away as Rincon in Ventura County, began to suffer sand deprivation.

Today, the harbor is the beautiful home to many pleasure craft and a small commercial fishing fleet. And Santa Barbara beaches are sandy and inviting. But this beauty and sand comes at a price: much dredging and expense is continually needed to keep the harbor mouth open, the beaches supplied with sand.

This walk explores West Beach and the marina, as well as Shoreline Park. An optional return route points out some of the Spanish Mission-revival-style architecture that drew —and still draws—visitors to Santa Barbara.

DIRECTIONS: Begin at the foot of Stearns Wharf where State Street meets Cabrillo Boulevard.

MTD: Downtown/Waterfront Shuttle to Stearns Wharf. Line 16, travels on Cabrillo Blvd, between Castillo and Loma Alta.

THE WALK: Saunter up-coast along the beach or on the sidewalk along Cabrillo Boulevard. Near the end of the beach, at the corner of Castillo and Cabrillo (an example of those similar-sounding Spanish street names that drive visitors mad!) is Los Banos del Mar, site of the municipal pool and the kiddie pool for the under-seven set.

Head for the water now. You'll spot Sea Landing, a small dock that serves as headquarters for charter fishing boats and a boat launching facility. Join the walkway that leads along the marina, where a diversity of pleasure craft are moored. The ocean beyond the breakwater might look tranquil; however, for the sailor, the rough seas and unpredictable weather of the Santa Barbara Channel can provide quite a challenge to seamanship.

At the breakwater, turn left and walk past the former U.S. Naval Reserve building, now home to seafood restaurants, and the Santa Barbara Martime Museum with interpretive displays about local marine history and science. Exhibits lead visitors on a path through maritime history starting from the seafaring Chumash and encompassing present day environmental concerns. Take the elevator to an observation room on the fourth floor for great clear day vistas of the town and harbor. Here you'll find the Outdoors Santa Barbara Visitor Center, a multi-agency staffed outpost offering information about Los Padres National Forest, the National Park Service and Channel Islands National Park, as well as local parks and preserves.

Continue past restaurants, yacht brokers, a marine supply store and an unloading dock for the fishing fleet. At day's end, you can often watch the fishermen unload their catch from the boats onto trucks. About 90 percent of Southern California's abalone and shrimp come from the Channel. Buy fresh catch for dinner at the Fisherman's Market.

Continue along the harborside walkway to a plaque commemorating Santa Barbara's commercial fishing fleet, and to a statue of a boy riding a seahorse donated by Santa Barbara's sister city of Puerto Vallarta. To the right is the Santa Barbara Yacht Club. Members get great sunset views from the club's twin wraparound decks. Non-members get their views from out on the breakwater.

Walk out onto the breakwater, which horseshoe-curves around to the east to protect the harbor. Along the harbor side of the breakwater are flags representing various Santa Barbara civic and community service groups. If it's a windy day. hold onto your hat! Sometimes when the wind whips the ocean, saltwater sprays over the sea wall and douses breakwater walkers. The breakwater can be an exciting walk when a storm is rising!

If you want to explore more of Santa Barbara's waterfront, return to the vicinity of the yacht club and follow Leadbetter Beach, or cut through the parking lot if you insist, toward Santa Barbara Point. Leadbetter Beach is largely a manufactured creation; construction of the harbor caused a large amount of sand to be deposited here. Above you, across Cabrillo Boulevard, is Santa Barbara City College.

A sidewalk leads you up to Shoreline Park, a grassy strip along La Mesa Bluff overlooking the Pacific. Picnicking, kite-flying and whale-watching (in winter) are popular park activities.

For a glimpse of Santa Barbara's beachfront architecture, past and present, return to the infamous Castillo/Cabrillo intersection, and walk

Buy fresh catch-of-the-day at Fisherman's Market at the breakwater.

back toward the wharf along the north (mountain) side of Cabrillo Boulevard.

A short distance away is palm-lined Ambassador Park, where a plaque commemorates Burton Mound, one of Santa Barbara's most significant archeological sites. Here stood the Chumash village of Syukhtun, "where two trails run," and a burial site. At one time, the 30-foot high, 600-foot by 500-foot mound belonged to former fur trader Lewis Burton, who was elected Santa Barbara's first American mayor in 1850.

Milo M. Potter made a molehill out of the mound when he built his opulent Potter Hotel in 1902. The Mission Revival-style hotel featured a telephone in every room. It was destroyed by fire in 1921.

All mourned the Potter's passing of the hotel property except archeologists, who dug up many Chumash artifacts before all but this small park was subdivided. The double row of palm trees, which once lined the promenade leading to the hotel entrance, are all that remain of the Potter Hotel.

Spanish Revival architecture fans will want to meander through the park to the pleasant side streets near Cabrillo Boulevard. Mixed in with the motels are small courts and residences that reflect both the best of this architecture and some absolutely kitschy knock-offs.

Before returning to Stearns Wharf, take a peek at Villa Rosa at 15 Chapala Street, a breathtaking example of Spanish Colonial Revival architecture. The former Belvedere Apartments, now a bed-and-breakfast, is a gem of a building.

Chumash Point
Santa Barbara City College

Take a walk through one of the nation's most beautifully situated community colleges and enjoy spectacular coastal views from atop the campus bluffs. With its excellent academic programs and attractive setting, Santa Barbara City College attracts students from across the nation.

Chumash Point Ethnobotanical Preserve displays the regional flora that sustained the native Chumash for many, many generations. A self-guided trail leads through assemblages of herbs, shrubs, vines and trees typical of the kind of plant life that characterized coastal Chumash lands, a territory that extended from the Ventura River up-coast to Point Conception.

The preserve was designed by the college's Environmental Horticulture Department. Students care for the preserve's plants and are gradually implementing a plan to restore all native flora atop the college's bluffs. It's good practice for students working toward a two-year AS degree in "Regenerative and Restoration Horticulture."

The Chumash built fine ocean-going canoes and paddled to the four northern Channel Islands. Island plant life from San Miguel, Santa Rosa, Santa Cruz and Anacapa islands greets walkers on the first segment of the interpretive trail. Look for the island oak, island tree mallow, island bush poppy, island Bishop pine and, of course, look out at the islands themselves, floating so enticingly on the horizon.

The identification signs by the plants are sometimes in poor condition, or missing altogether. However, the path itself is usually in good shape. And the clear-day vistas are marvelous!

The blufftop path meanders through several more coastal habitats including coastal sage, dunes, chaparral, riparian and forest. Near trail's end above Castillo Point, you'll find Torrey pines (which survive only in a state preserve north of San Diego and on Santa Rosa Island) and enjoy spectacular views of the Santa Barbara Harbor and many miles of coastline.

Directions: On the weekends you'll probably be able to find parking on campus, but on a weekday during the school session, forget it. Park in the one of the beach lots across from Santa Barbara City College and walk up the hill to the start of the trail, located above the sports stadium.

Walk up the stairs and paved pathways to the left (west) of the stadium. Once atop the bluffs, head to mthe right past some small science buildings and a parking lot to the start of the trail.

Thousand Steps
Thousand Steps Trail

Thousand Steps to Arroyo Burro County Park is 4 miles round trip.

A long stairwell, but nowhere near a thousand steps, leads to the beach just upcoast from Shoreline Park. Much to the frustration of coastal activists and a thousand walkers, the city closed venerable Thousand Steps in 1992, citing high maintenance costs for the closure; it was reopened in 1996. This beach hike explores the strand below the tall bluffs of Santa Barbara's Mesa neighborhood and below the city's Douglas Family Preserve. Walk this narrow beach only at low tide.

The blufftop where you begin this walk is part of a marine terrace that includes Shoreline Park. Geologists call it a fault scarp that was created by movement along the Mesa Fault; scientists speculate that Santa Barbara's devastating 1925 earthquake was caused by movement along this fault.

Back of the beach is a hump of land separating downtown from the sea called "The Mesa." It's a Spanish word meaning table. Japanese farmers settled in this area and established nurseries and flower farms. By the 1920s, a Sunday drive out to the flower farms was a popular family outing. These days the Mesa is a mellow middle-class neighborhood, whose residents enjoy the access they have to both beach and town.

Directions: From Stearns Wharf at the foot of State Street, head west (upcoast) along Cabrillo Boulevard, which soon becomes Shoreline Drive and meanders past Shoreline Park. Park in the farthest west lot for Shoreline Park or continue until you reach Santa Cruz Boulevard which is not a boulevard at all, but a tiny residential street. Park along Shoreline Drive. Thousand Steps is at the coastal end of Santa Cruz Boulevard.

The Walk: Walk to the end of Santa Cruz Boulevard to the viewpoint. The Santa Barbara Lighthouse, located upcoast, was first lit in 1856 and was tended by Albert Williams and his wife, Julia, for forty years. Destroyed by the great Santa Barbara earthquake of 1925 it was replaced by an automated light.

Descend the steps to the beach and enjoy the solitude that the sandy and cobble beach usually brings. About a mile's hike brings you to the Mesa Lane Stairs, the only coastal access point between One Thousand Steps and Arroyo Burro County Park.

Continue another mile to the park. Park facilities, a restaurant and more miles of sandy beach are located across Arroyo Burro Creek. The creek mouth is usually easily fordable.

Channel Islands National Park

CONGRESS, IN ESTABLISHING Channel Islands National Park, did not intend it as a vacation spot for the comfort-loving, but rather as a preserve for what some scientists have called the "American Galapagos." Top priority was given to the protection of sea lions and seals, endemic plants like the Santa Cruz pine, rich archaeological digs, and what may be the final resting place of Portuguese navigator Juan Rodríguez Cabrillo, who explored the California coast for the Spanish crown in the 16th century.

Would-be adventurers enjoy the visitors center in Ventura Harbor as an exciting sneak preview of the splendid park out there in the Pacific, 12 to 60 miles away, a series of blue-tinged mountains floating on the horizon. The visitors center not only has island history and ecology exhibits, but provides up to the minute boat transportation information.

The Channel Islands parallel the Southern California coast, which at this point is running in a more or less east-west direction. In 1980, five of the eight Channel Islands—Anacapa, San Miguel, Santa Barbara, Santa Cruz and Santa Rosa—became America's fortieth national park. The waters surrounding the national park islands are protected as the Channel Islands National Marine Sanctuary.

The islands' even sea-tempered climate has preserved plants that either were altered through evolution on the mainland, or perished altogether at man's hand. What you see on the islands is Southern California of a millennium ago.

Because of the fragile islands ecology, hiking on the islands is more regulated than it is in most places. You must always stay on the trail, and on some islands be accompanied by a national park ranger or Nature Conservancy employee.

To arrange passage to the Channel Islands from Santa Barbara, call Truth Aquatics, an official National Park concessionaire. The company leads day trips and multi-day trips to the islands, particularly to Santa Cruz and Santa Rosa islands. If you'd like to fly to Santa Rosa Island, call another official park concessionaire, Channel Islands Aviation, located at the Camarillo Airport.

Douglas Family Preserve
Wilcox Trail

1-mile loop around preserve

For the walker, the attractions of Douglas Family Preserve are many. Cliff-hugging Monterey pine and cypress trees frame grand coastal views from Pt. Mugu to Gaviota. A lovely stand of coastal live oak borders the north side of preserve. In wintertime, migrating monarch butterflies cluster in a south side eucalyptus grove.

During the two decade-long struggle to preserve the coastal bluffs above Arroyo Burro Beach, conservationists sometimes called the disputed land "the last great place." Indeed the Wilcox Property, as its long been known by locals, was/is the largest area of coastal open space within the city limits of Santa Barbara.

In 1949, Roy Wilcox moved his large nursery from the east Los Angeles community of Montebello to Santa Barbara's bluffs. Azaleas, palms, and a wide variety of decorative indoor plants were grown on the fertile land, as well as in green houses, and shipped to market around the country.

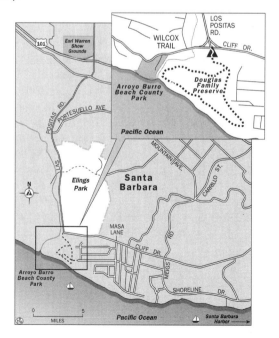

Soon after the nursery business closed in 1972, Santa Barbara residents formed a chapter of SWAP (Small Wilderness Area Preservation) and spearheaded an effort to create a park on the former Wilcox property. Developers, several of them in fact, had different ideas: a huge luxury hotel, a residential subdivision, and an upscale senior-housing project known as Cypress Point. In both 1987 and '88, Santa Barbara conservationists tried to convince their fellow citizens to set aside the property as a park, but failed (barely) in getting the necessary two-thirds majority at the polls.

Finally in 1996, in a truly grand display of community support, Santa Barbara residents raised more than $2 million in two months to help the Trust for Public Land purchase the Wilcox Property for $3.6 million. The property, now a city park, was named Douglas Family Preserve in recognition of actor Michael Douglas, who made a sizable contribution to help Santa Barbarans acquire the park land.

Visitors should be forewarned: This property has been designated as a leash-free park for dogs. Anyone who is fearful of canines should steer clear of this walk—it's become known as a place for dog-lovers only!

Directions: From Highway 101 in Santa Barbara, exit on Las Positas Road and follow it 1.5 miles south (toward the ocean) to its terminus at Cliff Drive. Turn right on Cliff Drive, then left into the parking lot for Arroyo Burro County Park. Park in the east lot (the one along Cliff Drive) and look for the trailhead at a gated fire road off Cliff Drive a short distance east of the parking lot.

To reach a second major preserve entry (and our preferred trailhead) follow Cliff Drive east (downcoast) to Mesa Lane. Turn right. Just before the lane reaches its end and the Mesa Lane coastal accessway, turn right on Medcliff Road and drive a couple blocks to the road's end at the Wilcox Preserve. Parking is along the nearby residential streets.

The Walk: If you begin from the Cliff Drive entry, you'll ascend the oak lined road to the blufftop. On a clockwise tour of the preserve you'll pass numerous palm trees, follow a wide path along the cliffs high (200 feet) above the beach below, and reach a dramatic vista point above Arroyo Burro Beach.

From whichever start point you choose, keep walking the preserve's perimeter to close the loop, or select a more interior trail. En route are numerous reminders of the old Wilcox nursery including towering bird-of-paradise and crumbling greenhouse foundations. Keen-eyed gardeners will enjoy identifying the many exotic plants that thrive in the preserve.

Arroyo Burro Beach
Arroyo Burro Trail

From Arroyo Burro Beach County Park to
Goleta Beach County Park is 5 miles one way

This beach hike begins at Arroyo Burro Beach County Park. At the turn of the 20th-century the Hendry family owned the beach and it was known as Hendry's. Today some Santa Barbarans refer to it as "Henry's." The beach was officially re-christened Arroyo Burro in 1947 when the state purchased it for $15,000. The park, later given to the county, was named for the creek that empties into the ocean at this point. Arroyo Burro is popular for picnicking, boogie boarding, sunbathing and hangglider watching. Don't miss the most recent attraction, the Southcoast Watershed Resource Center, a facility operated by the Community Environmental Council. Learn about creek and ocean environments from displays and interactive exhibits.

This is definitely a locals' beach—not by any deliberate effort on the part of Santa Barbarans to make it exclusive, but by the beach's location off the tourist track. Both Arroyo Burro Beach County Park and Goleta Beach County Park have waterside cafés so beach hikers may begin or end their jaunt with a meal or drink. If you can arrange a car shuttle, this walk is an ideal one-way outing.

Walk at low tide. A rocky point located a mile downcoast from Goleta Pier is difficult to surmount except at low tide.

On the bluffs above the beach is one of the most unique residential communities in America. "Sun-kissed, ocean-washed, mountain-girded, island-guarded" was the breathless description of Hope Ranch gushing forth from real estate brochures of the 1920s. In this case, the agents were offering more truth than hype. Hope Ranch was—and still is—one of the most naturally blessed residential areas on the West Coast. Residents often ride their horses along the surf line.

Directions: From Highway 101 in Santa Barbara, exit on Las Positas Road and drive south to its intersection with Cliff Drive and make a right. Arroyo Burro Beach County Park is a short distance on your left.

You can use the MTD bus to return to the trailhead.

MTD: Mesa/La Cumbre line stops at Arroyo Burro Beach.

The Walk: Head upcoast on Arroyo Burro Beach. The area was once the site of a major Chumash village. Archeological excavations have produced many tools and artifacts.

You'll round a minor point and after two miles or so of beach-walking, pass the red-tiled changing rooms of Hope Ranch Beach Club.

More Mesa Beach follows, one of the most peaceful beaches in the county. Only the buzzing of innumerable flies around the kelp disturbs the tranquility of the serious sunworshippers who bake their hides here. The only public accessway is the dirt path and stairway leading up to More Mesa.

Beyond More Mesa is another mile of sandy, kelp-strewn beach. The sea cliffs here and in other parts of Santa Barbara have receded three to ten inches per year or roughly 50 feet per century. While this erosion is less than other parts of the world—the White Cliffs of Dover, for example—it's still substantial enough to be a consideration for builders of bluff-top houses.

No, that's not a lighthouse you see in the distance. It's Storke Tower in the center of the University of California at Santa Barbara. As you walk Goleta Beach, you'll round the point and see Goleta Pier.

In 1981, five ancient cannons were found along Goleta Beach, a half-mile south of Goleta Slough. Pacific storms exhumed the circa 1700s' cannons. Historians speculate the cannons are from British ships, which once lurked along the coast waiting for the treasure-laden galleons of the Spanish.

Beach hikers soon arrive at the mouth of Goleta Slough, large tidal mudflats that lie between the UCSB campus and the Santa Barbara Airport. Atascadero Creek empties into the slough, where a great variety of birds, crustaceans and native flora thrive.

Although the slough is smaller than it was before bulldozing and flood control projects, in the 1960s it was saved from a Santa Barbara mayor's pet plan: a speedboat lake surrounded by a racetrack for sports cars.

Wade the shallow, sandy-bottomed slough, resume walking on the sandy beach, and enter Goleta Beach County Park. Goleta Pier's 1,450-foot length is a nice walk in and of itself. It's a popular sport-fishing spot. A restaurant and picnic area are located near the pier.

Unpack your picnic, unroll your beach towel and catch some rays, or walk upcoast to nearby UCSB.

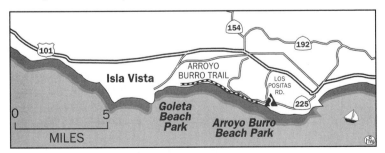

More Mesa
More Mesa Trail

1 mile to beach; 3.5-mile loop around mesa

Ask locals about More Mesa and watch the expression on their faces—a smile, a frown, a wink. Smiles will come from those who've found tranquility roaming the bluffs of More Mesa. Frowns may darken the faces of some; developers and their supporters have long wanted to build housing on the mesa and resent the efforts of conservationists and county officials to preserve the land.

The winks might come from those who know that the isolated beach below More Mesa is one of Santa Barbara's secrets; clean, mellow and, for some sun worshippers, *au naturel.*

The mesa was part of a large spread, Rancho La Goleta, when rancher Thomas More bought 400 acres in 1857 and began grazing cattle on the land. An enterprising fellow, More noticed natural tar seeping from mesa cliffs, gathered it up and sold it to San Francisco, where the asphaltum was used to pave city streets in the 1860s.

Today, the mesa is known for other natural resources—primarily its bird life. Black-shouldered kites forage the mesa. The population of this bird is on the rebound after habitat destruction and egg collection nearly caused its extinction at the turn of the century.

Other rare birds include the northern harrier and the merlin (a kind of falcon). To the chagrin of developers, the rare, migratory short-eared owl winters on the mesa. "The short-eared owl doesn't pay taxes," scoffed one developer, whose project was delayed because of environmental concerns.

Naturally, the one-mile walk across More Mesa to the cliff edge, then down a steep path to the beach, is a winner on a sunny day. But don't overlook More Mesa when the weather is bad; its quiet can be enjoyed on the darkest of days.

You can also enjoy More Mesa without going down to the beach. The property is honeycombed with trails. Walk around the mesa on winter evenings during the hour before sunset. The black-shouldered kite, marsh hawk and other raptors are quite active in their pursuit of food.

Directions: From upper State Street at its junction with Highway 154, continue along State as it becomes Hollister 1.2 miles to Puente Drive. Turn left and drive 0.75 mile to Via Huerto on your left. Park along Puente Drive, which is known as Vieja Drive just past Via Huerto.

MTD: Line 6 State/Hollister stops at about Hollister and Puente Drive.

A second way to enter More Mesa is to continue a short distance along Vieja Drive and walk up Mockingbird Lane to the mesa.

The Walk: From Via Huerto, join the dirt path as it ascends steeply for a hundred yards to a wooden fence and row of cypress trees. The path then descends to the relatively flat mesa itself. As you'll notice on your right, not all attempts to keep More Mesa pristine were successful; there are two housing developments on the mesa's northeast corner. The path, joined by other paths connecting from the west, cross the sweet-smelling, fennel-covered flatlands. Mustard predominates and in springtime covers the bluffs with a blanket of yellow.

At the ocean edge of the mesa is a line of eucalyptus and the dirt path leading down to the beach. The steep path is stabilized by logs. At the bottom is More Mesa Beach, where sunbathers can spread their towels and doze and beach walkers can travel as far up or down the coast as time and tides permit.

Hikers will definitely enjoy the blufftop path leading upcoast along the oceanside edge of More Mesa. The path offers great views of the campus of the University of California at Santa Barbara.

Continue on a clockwise route around the periphery of More Mesa. Follow the bluff trail to the first major trail on your right, turning north toward the mountains, then dipping into oak-filled ravines. You'll pass some minor trails then intersect the old Southern Pacific railroad bed; the railroad crossed the mesa in 1887. Beneath the rail route today is a pipeline that carries natural gas from nearby deposits discovered in the 1930s. And the old rail route is a fine hiking trail. A left on the trail will take you through oak woodland to Shoreline Drive and Orchid Drive in a residential area. A right on the trail leads through the oaks along seasonal Atascadero Creek. The "pipeline trail" eventually intersects a profusion of trails. Improvise a route eastward back across the mesa to the trailhead.

Ellwood Beach

From Goleta Beach to Coal Oil Preserve is 7 miles round trip;
to Ellwood Beach Pier is 12 miles round trip

Around seven o'clock in the evening of February 23, 1942, while most Americans were listening to President Roosevelt's fireside chat on the radio, strange explosions were heard near Goleta. In the first attack on U.S. soil since the War of 1812, a Japanese submarine surfaced off the rich oilfield on Ellwood Beach, twelve miles upcoast from Santa Barbara, and lobbed sixteen shells into the tidewater field.

"Their marksmanship was poor," asserted Lawrence Wheeler, proprietor of a roadside inn near the oil fields. Most observers agreed with Wheeler, who added there was no panic among his dinner patrons. "We immediately blacked out the place," he said.

The Japanese gunners were presumably aiming at the oil installations and the coast highway bridge over the Southern Pacific tracks. Tokyo claimed the raid "a great military success" though the incredibly bad marksmen managed to inflict only $500 worth of damage.

The walk along Goleta Beach to Ellwood Oil Field is interesting for more than historical reasons. On the way to the oilfield–battlefield, you'll pass tidepools, shifting sand dunes, and the Devereux Slough. The slough is a unique intertidal ecosystem and is protected for teaching and research purposes by Coal Oil Point Preserve.

Directions: From Highway 101 in Goleta, head south on Ward Memorial Drive (Route 217) for two miles to Goleta Beach County Park. Park in the large beach lot.

MTD: Line #18, the Goleta Loop stops on Hollister near Santa Barbara Shores.

The Walk: Proceed upcoast and in a quarter-mile you'll reach a stretch of coast called the Main Campus Reserve Area, where you'll find the Goleta Slough. The same month the Japanese bombed Ellwood Beach, Santa Barbara voters approved a bond issue to buy land around Goleta Slough, and a modern airport was constructed on the site of the old cow pasture–airfield. The slough, host to native and migratory waterfowl, is a remnant of a wetland that was once more extensive.

Continue up-beach past the handsome sandstone cliffs. Occasionally a high tide may force you to detour atop the bluffs through the UCSB campus to avoid getting wet. A mile and a half from the county park, you'll round Goleta Point and head due west. You pass a nice tidepool area; judging from the number of college students, it is well studied.

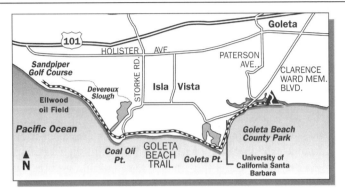

Two more miles of beachcombing brings you to Coal Oil Point. You'll want to explore the nature reserve here. (Please observe all posted warnings; this is a very fragile area.)

The dunes are the first component of the reserve encountered on the seaward side. Sandy hillocks are stabilized with grasses and rushes. Salty sand provides little nourishment yet the hardy seaside flora manage to survive, settling at close to the water as the restless Pacific will permit. The dunes keep the plants from blowing away and the plants return the favor for the dunes.

Pick up the trail over the dunes on the east side of the reserve. The fennel-lined trail passes under the cypress trees and climbs a bluff above the slough to a road on the reserve's perimeter. It's a good place to get "the big picture" of the slough, a unique ecosystem. Something like an estuary, a slough has a mixture of fresh and salt water, but an estuary has a more stable mixture. The water gets quite salty at Devereux Slough, with little freshwater flushing.

At the slough, birdwatchers rhapsodize over snowy egrets and great blue herons, black-bellied plovers and western sandpipers. Avid bird watchers flock to the slough for birdathons—bird-sighting competitions.

Return to the beach and continue walking up the coast. In two miles you'll pass under an old barnacle-covered oil drilling platform and enter Ellwood Oil Field. Here the Japanese fired shots heard 'round the world—and missed.

Monarch Butterflies

Every fall, millions of monarch butterflies migrate south to the damp coastal woodlands of Central and Southern California. The monarch's awe-inspiring migration and formation of what entomologists call over-wintering colonies are two of nature's most colorful autumn events.

The butterflies seem to have a knack for wintering in some of California's most beautiful coastal locales. In Santa Barbara County, the monarchs flock to the eucalyptus groves above Ellwood Beach and around Lake Los Carneros. Monarchs are also attracted to El Capitan State Beach and, in lesser numbers, to other locations along Santa Barbara's shores.

Monarchs hang on trees in thick bunches, resembling so many triangular dead brown leaves until, warmed by the sun, they spread their wings and fly around the aptly-named butterfly groves. This is fall color, California-style, an autumn spectacle that lingers well into winter and stays in a visitor's heart for a very long time.

About August, great groups of monarchs from Wyoming, Montana, southern Canada and other locales west of the Rockies begin their long journey to wintering grounds in the Golden State. Arrival and departure times, as well as population sizes, vary from year to year and from locale to locale, but generally speaking the butterflies make it to the California coast in mid-October and may stay until mid-February, or even March.

While monarchs begin life as caterpillars, there's nothing sluggish about their pace. Monarchs have been known to fly as far as 2,000 miles, and as fast as 30 miles an hour at a cruising altitude of 1,000 feet.

How monarchs determine where to go remains a mystery. Do they follow food sources? Scents? Is it all instinct? Do they operate with some kind of celestial navigation? The mystery is all the more baffling because no single monarch completes a round trip.

The female monarch lays her eggs on milkweed plants. A couple of days later, caterpillars emerge and feed voraciously for two weeks. Each caterpillar then forms a chrysalis (similar to a cocoon) and attaches itself upside down to a twig. After about two weeks of metamorphosis, the caterpillar is transformed into a butterfly and joins the return northward migration of its parents.

The monarch's evolutionary success lies not only in its unique ability to migrate to warmer climes, but in its mastery of chemical warfare. The butterfly feeds on milkweed—the favored poison of

assassins during the Roman Empire. The milkweed diet makes the monarch toxic to birds; after munching a monarch or two and becoming sick, they learn to leave the butterflies alone.

The butterflies advertise their poisonous nature with their conspicuous coloring. They have brownish-red wings with black veins. Outer wing edges are dark brown with white and yellow spots. While one might assume the monarch's startling coloration would make them easy prey for predators, just the opposite is true; bright colors in nature are often a warning that a creature is toxic or distasteful.

Monarchs are excellent field thermometers. When the temperature exceeds 55 degrees F., the monarchs flit about on branches and fly around seeking nectar. However, if its colder than 55 degrees F., rainy or very damp, the monarchs cluster together in trees for warmth, and for protection from the wind and rain.

While the monarchs' arrival is usually a fairly predictable natural phenomenon—at least in comparison to California's notoriously fickle wildflower displays—call the relevant park or preserve for a monarch update before you make a butterfly pilgrimage.

Santa Barbara Shores County Park
Santa Barbara Shores Trail
3.5-mile loop; longer and shorter options available

This may just be the best of what's left of California's south coast: a mosaic of grasslands, vernal pools and some of the nation's best monarch butterfly groves—all linked with an enticing network of footpaths that serves up stunning views of the Santa Ynez Mountains, Channel Islands and wide blue Pacific.

It may not be left for long, however. Development pressures, from both the private sector (a proposed suburban subdivision) and the public sector (a proposed sports complex) threaten to overwhelm the blufftops located adjacent to the campus of the University of California at Santa Barbara.

The beaches, bluffs and residential community located a dozen miles upcoast from downtown Santa Barbara go by the names of Ellwood Beach and Santa Barbara Shores. At issue are the blufftops, owned by three landowners with very different agendas: the county parks department, Southwest Diversified (the developer) and a university-administered nature preserve.

While the project(s) are not likely to break ground anytime soon, a lot of ground will be broken if developments proceed as planned. The concerned citizen need only check out the instant suburbs mushrooming opposite this coast on the inland side of Highway 101 to be able to imagine what's in store for Santa Barbara Shores.

Should developments proceed, much of the area's trail system will remain intact; however, the face of Santa Barbara Shores will change considerably. We suggest hiking this land in its natural state while you still can.

Hiking from Santa Barbara Shores County Park to UCSB is a special experience indeed. From the trailhead, the hiker takes inspiration from a half-mile wide grassland extending to the edge of the sea cliffs. In winter and spring, the various grasses are a palette of greens dotted with shallow, shimmering pools. In summer and autumn, the grasses turn shades of amber gold and russet. Among the splendors in the grass are several native species including abundant purple needlegrass, as well as blue-eyed grass, California brome and owl's clover.

Scattered atop the bluffs are about two-dozen vernal pools, topographical depressions that attract unique flora able to adapt to alternating wet and dry periods. Coyote thistle, wooly heads and popcorn flower are some of the plants encircling these ecological rarities.

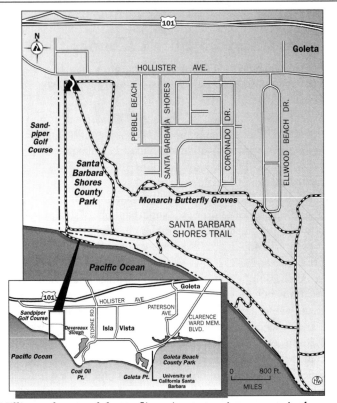

Millions of monarch butterflies migrate to winter roosts in the eucalyptus woodlands that border the inland side of Santa Barbara Shores. Scientists rate these groves as among the three largest overwintering sites west of the Rockies. The Land Trust of Santa Barbara County recently purchased a portion of the butterflies' roosting area for a nature preserve.

The bluffs, popular with university students and horseback riders since the 1960s, have an excellent, though mostly unsigned, trail system. For a first-time visit, we suggest a counter-clockwise loop out to the coast and a return via the butterfly groves. Ambitious hikers can continue on blufftop trails to the student-populated community of Isla Vista at the fringe of the UCSB campus.

Directions: From Highway 101, some 12 miles upcoast from downtown Santa Barbara, take the Glen Annie Road/ Storke Road exit. Turn left on Storke Road and drive to the first intersection. Turn right on Hollister Avenue and proceed 1.6 miles to an unsigned turnoff on the left (coast) side of the road. Turn left into the dirt parking lot of Santa Barbara Shores County Park. (If you see Sandpiper Golf Course on your

left as you're motoring along Hollister Avenue, you overshot the park turnoff.)

MTD: Line 23 Winchester Canyon/Ellwood bus stops on Hollister Avenue near the Sandpiper Golf Course.

The Walk: Choose either the straight-toward-shore west trail that leads alongside a eucalyptus windbreak and Sandpiper Golf Course or a signed path that cuts diagonally across county park land toward the shore. Both paths traverse grasslands and intersect a bluff edge trail in about 0.6 mile.

Head downcoast atop the 60 to 80-foot high cliffs, which are cloaked in buckwheat, sage, lemonade berry mustard and fennel. A half-mile's travel brings you to a junction with a major beach access trail. (You can walk this beach to the university, but beware that it's among the state's tar-iest and you won't get far before black goo gloms onto your shoes.)

Continue another 0.25 mile across the bluffs to a line of eucalyptus trees and join a north-trending trail that follows the trees inland. The view to the right (east) is dominated by two towers—UCSB's 175-foot Storke Tower, tallest structure in Santa Barbara County, and Santa Barbara Airport's new control tower.

As you near the residential area of Santa Barbara Shores, you'll encounter a confusion of paths meandering amidst the eucalyptus. Head toward the end of these residential cul-de-sacs and a bit to your left (west) until you intersect the major east-west footpath through the eucalyptus groves. Head left on this path through butterfly country, over a forest floor strewn with thick layers of bark and leaves. Emerging from the eucalyptus, you'll intersect the county park's main trail that will return you to the trailhead.

Haskell's Beach and Bacara Resort
Haskell's Beach Trail

From Bacara Resort to Dos Pueblos Canyon is 5.5 miles round trip

For decades, Haskell's was a locals-only beach, a secret surf spot, a strand located off the Santa Barbara tourist track and far from its many restaurants and hotels.

Enter the Bacara Resort and Spa, a $220 million development that's been widely advertised across the nation and around the world. As a result of this upscale marketing campaign, the beach is fast becoming an international attraction.

For more than a decade, Haskell's Beach was the subject of a dispute between the resort builder and local conservationists. Now that the resort is here to stay, conservationists are directing their efforts toward a much larger issue—creation of Gaviota National Seashore, which would place many miles of beach upcoast from the Bacara Resort under National Park Service protection.

The resort seems to be trying to present an air of privacy and exclusivity for its guests while, at the same time, sharing a beach that's been public for generations. Local surfers continue to ride the waves while hotel guests surf the web from fully wired, high-speed internet-connected poolside cabañas.

Long, romantic walks on beautiful beaches—and time to enjoy it all.

The stunning, Spanish-revival style resort, which occupies a commanding position on the bluffs overlooking the beach, features 360 rooms, three swimming pools and a luxurious, state-of-the-art spa. Not all of Bacara's buildings are reserved for its guests. The resort just finished constructing some first-class public amenities—deluxe restrooms and outdoor showers, as well as a handsome little play area and picnic ground with tables that overlook the beach.

However, next to all this beauty is a real beast—Venoco's Ellwood Plant, an oil-and-gas-processing facility. This plumber's nightmare of a plant is not visible from the beach, but it is an appallingly ugly greeting to beach- and Bacara-bound motorists, despite the resort's efforts to landscape it out of view.

A great beach hike awaits those who stride upcoast from the resort. Beyond the Bacara extends a deserted, mostly undeveloped coastline. If conservationists prevail in their efforts, this coastline will one day be placed under National Park Service protection as Gaviota National Seashore.

Birdwatching is particularly good along this beach. Squadrons of pelicans rest on the reefs and swoop low over the water. Harbor seals haul out on the beach for a snooze.

Walking two or three miles up the coast from the Bacara is a delight—as long as you remember to consult a local tide table and walk at low tide. This beach hike is best started about two hours before low tide and best finished two hours after low tide. At higher tides, you may encounter difficult, unsafe and even downright impassable conditions.

Dabs and globs of tar on the rocks and sand can be a minor nuisance to the beachcomber. Oil companies say "natural seepage" accounts for the tar while conservationists point their fingers at the oil drilling platforms in the Santa Barbara Channel.

Directions: From northbound Highway 101. Some 12 miles upcoast from downtown Santa Barbara, exit on Storke Road and go left 0.4 mile to Hollister Avenue. Turn right (west) and drive 2 miles. Veer left toward the entrance of the Sandpiper Golf Course onto the Bacara Resort access road and proceed 0.5 mile. Several hundred yards short of the main resort complex, turn left at the public beach access sign and into the public parking area above the beach.

MTD: Line 23 Winchester Canyon/Ellwood stops on Hollister near Sandpiper Golf Course.

The Walk: Descend to the beach and soon cross the shallow mouth of a creek. Sycamore, oak, cottonwood and willow line the banks of the Tecolote Creek, which meanders down the coastal slopes of the Santa Ynez Mountains. Most months it's a mellow watercourse but the creek can rise and get a bit more spirited during the November through April

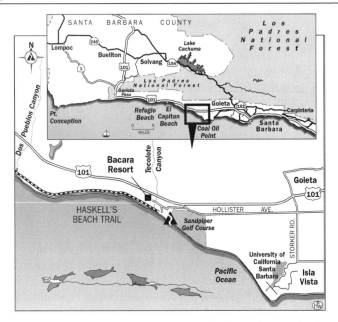

rainy season. A brackish lagoon is habitat for the endangered tidewater goby and the Southwestern pond turtle.

Pass below the resort, which looks a bit like a giant wedding cake from the beach hiker's point of view, and reach the Venoco Pier. It's not difficult to envision this industrial pier transformed from loading facility to romantic promenade. Imagine a bistro at pier's end with inspiring views of the Santa Ynez Mountains, the resort, the university and the Channel Islands. . . . For now, however, it's very much private property and off-limits to beach hikers.

Not far upcoast from the pier, the beachcomber rounds a little cove and reaches a hundred yard-long series of rock reefs. Tidepools lie hidden in what resemble long, narrow and very shallow gullies.

About a mile from the resort, the beach opens up and it's easy to feel like you're the only one around for miles—which, on a weekday, might very well be the case. Fluted cliff bottoms have some cave-like recesses where you can find shade or a picnic spot out of the wind.

Trail's end for all but the most intrepid beach hikers is the creek flowing through Dos Pueblos Canyon to the ocean. For many generations the native Chumash had villages here. It's a nice place to relax before heading back downcoast.

Gaviota Coast

EXTENDING FROM Goleta's newest subdivisions to the Santa Barbara-San Luis Obispo county line is the Gaviota Coast, 50 miles of coast that resembles the state's golden shores of the 19th century. Cows graze the grassy coastal plain, red-tailed hawks ride the thermals above the Santa Ynez Mountains, dolphins swim and dive in the great blue Pacific. Only mighty waves thundering against all-but-deserted shores break a silence that is all too rare in Southern California. This silence, these mountains, these shores are in danger, threatened by a tidal wave of 21st century development. Greater Santa Barbara now extends a dozen or so miles upcoast from downtown to the edge of Goleta, a rapidly growing area complete with big box retail complexes, UCSB and 20,000 college students, the busy Santa Barbara Airport, a rapidly growing cluster of high-tech businesses known collectively as Silicon Beach and mushrooming subdivisions. If present trends continue, it won't be long before the Gaviota Coast becomes Greater Goleta.

Fortunately the Gaviota Coast has many friends and a growing national recognition. Many conservationists, politicians, scientists and park experts say the Gaviota Coast is of national parkland quality and ought to be preserved as Gaviota Coast National Seashore.

Protection of this coast as national parkland is the chief goal of the Gaviota Coast Conservancy, a group working to secure the cooperation of ranchers oil companies and assorted governmental land stewards including Los Padres National Forest and the state Department of Parks and Recreation. The group has compiled an impressive list of area's natural and historical resources.

Archaeologists have determined that the Gaviota Coast was home to the native Chumash for several thousand years and to Spanish, Mexican and American settlements for several hundred years.

Meteorologists say the Gaviota Coast is the place where the cool, moist climate of Northern California mixes and mingles with the drier, warmer climate of Southern California. This mixture creates a unique climate, one that nurtures biodiversity.

Unique plant and animal species survive in the area's sandstone bluffs, canyons and grasslands. Biologists call this ecological meeting place a biogeographic transition zone and regard it as one of the most impressive of such zones on the continent.

"Gaviota Coast National Seashore" would be a worthy addition to our nation's national parklands.

El Capitan, Refugio State Beaches
El Capitan Beach Trail

From El Capitan to Refugio State Beach is 6 miles round trip

Monarch butterflies and mellow beaches are the highlights of this coast walk north of Santa Barbara. Autumn, when the crowds have thinned and the butterflies have arrived, is a particularly fine time to roam the coast from El Capitan State Beach to Refugio State Beach.

El Capitan is a narrow beach at the mouth of El Capitan Creek. Shading the creek is a woodland of coast live oak and sycamore. During autumn, monarch butterflies congregate and breed in the trees here. (Ask park rangers where the monarchs cluster.)

"El Capitán" refers to Captain José Francisco de Ortega, a rotund Spanish Army officer who served as trail scout for the Portolá expedition. When he retired from service to the Crown in 1795, he owed the army money and offered to square things by raising cattle. The government granted him his chosen land: a coastal strip, two miles wide and twenty-five miles long extending from just east of Pt. Conception to Refugio Canyon. He called his land *Nuestra Señora del Refugio,* "Our Lady of Refuge." Alas, Captain Ortega's retirement was short-lived; he died three years later and was buried at the Santa Barbara Mission.

After the death of El Capitán, the Ortega family continued living in Refugio Canyon for many years. The mouth of the canyon at the Pacific was the major contraband-loading point for Southern California during the early years of the 19th century when Spanish settlers were forbidden to trade with Americans. From the Ortega Ranch, hides, tallow, leather goods and wine were loaded onto Boston-bound sailing ships.

Smuggling activity came to an end in 1818 when French Captain (some would say pirate) Hippoloyte de Bouchard sailed by. Bouchard, a mercenary hired by the Argentines, then struggling for independence against Spain, put ashore and burned Ortega's ranch buildings to the ground.

Beach, bluff and bike trails link El Capitan and Refugio state beaches. Depending on the tide, you can usually travel upcoast along El Capitan State Beach as far as Coral Canyon Beach. Then you can join the bluff trails or the bike path, which is also open to hikers, for the balance of the trip to Refugio State Beach.

El Capitan and Refugio are popular beach campgrounds and nice places to spend a weekend. Each beach boasts a small camp store (open

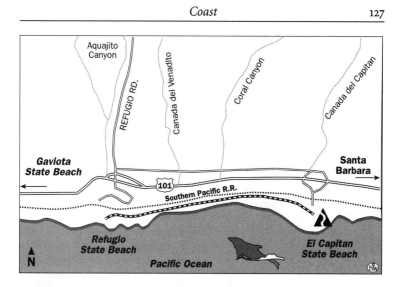

summer days and weekends only during other seasons), so refreshments are available on both ends of your beach walk.

Directions: From Highway 101, 19 miles upcoast from Santa Barbara, take the El Capitan State Beach exit. Park in one of the day use areas; the park day use fee is also honored at Refugio and Gaviota State Beaches.

The Walk: Descend one of the paths or staircases to the shore, then head upcoast along the mixed sandy and rocky beach. Sea cliffs are steep here because they are constantly being cut back by wave erosion. You'll pass wide Coral Canyon, its walls covered with beds of highly deformed light-colored shales.

At Coral Beach, the tides often discourage beach-walking, so head up to the bluffs and follow the bike path.

On the approach to Refugio State Beach, look for abundant kelp just offshore. If a breeze is blowing over the water, note how areas with kelp are smooth and kelp-less areas are rippled.

Refugio State Beach, at the mouth of Refugio Canyon, is a rocky beach with tidepools. Turn around here, or continue beach-walking upcoast (it's 10 more miles to Gaviota State Beach) for as long as time and tides permit.

El Capitan Canyon
Canyon and Ridgetop Trails

2 to 5 miles or more round trip

Before discussing the canyon's trails, it's imperative to mention the canyon's turnaround.

What a turnaround!

The El Capitan Canyon of the 1970s, '80s and '90s was a private, drive-in camp with scores of RVs lumbering down the narrow canyon road and parked door handle to door handle in the campground. A constant chorus of barking dogs added to the stress of a canyon crammed with as many as 3,000 people on a busy weekend.

Enter a new millennium, a new management philosophy, and new owners. The crowded camp was replaced with deluxe safari tents and cozy cabins with beds, linens and bathrooms. Yurts were constructed for group meetings or company conferences and an upscale camp store opened, stocked with an array of healthy foods and snacks.

In 1976, the state's Department of Parks and Recreation considered the purchase of the 3,150-acre El Capitan Ranch, but decided the owner (Texaco) was asking too steep a price, and the land itself was too steep and too inland. The state, with considerable assistance from the San Francisco-based Trust for Public Land, recently made arrangements to acquire some 2,500 acres of the property from two Santa Barbara developers who purchased the land in 1999.

Under terms of the sale, the developers will retain the campground and 650 acres of the property near Highway 101, where they intend to create a few lots for estate homes. The remaining acreage will be state parkland.

Once El Capitan Ranch is in the state park system, hikers will have access to the dramatic coastal slopes of the Santa Ynez Mountains via a nine-mile loop that follows old ranch roads. The route ascends to the ridgeline of the mountains and connects to routes in Los Padres National Forest.

El Capitan is now car-free thanks to a requirement that guests park at the entrance and use a shuttle service to reach overnight lodging. A no-pet policy means the canyon is blessedly quiet day and night, and the native wildlife is returning to reclaim long-lost habitat.

Guided kayak trips and mountain bike rides, a kids camp, rock-climbing outings and surfing lessons are among the activities available

Hikers await the fate of this land.

at El Capitan Canyon. Guests can join a naturalist led hike or explore the (as yet unsigned and unmapped) canyon trail network on their own.

Bordered on the south by El Capitan State Beach and on the north by Los Padres National Forest, the 3,000-acre El Capitan Ranch has the potential to become a hiker's paradise. Some 15 miles of old ranch roads weave through the property and are available for hiking. Paths lead alongside El Capitan Creek and ascend the ridges above El Capitan Canyon. Coastal views are absolutely stunning.

Local hikers would like to see the creation of more footpaths, as well as connector trails to link already existing dirt roads; these trail additions would enable the hiker to make loop trips of varying lengths.

Trails that link the mountains and shoreline are few and far between, so coastal hikers would surely support the vision of a path ascending from the beach, up El Capitan Canyon to the crest of the Santa Ynez Mountains near Broadcast Peak. That would be quite a day hike!

Directions: From Santa Barbara, drive 18 miles up-coast on Highway 101. Take the El Capitan State Beach and turn inland, following the signs to the entry kiosk in El Capitan Canyon.

Trail access and trailheads will be changing quite a bit in the months and years to come. The prudent hiker will phone El Capitan Canyon and/or El Capitan State Beach and get the definitive word on trails, parking requirements and fees.

Arroyo Hondo Preserve

A deep sandstone gorge cut by the Arroyo Hondo "Deep Stream" is the highlight of a new preserve on the Gaviota Coast. The 782-acre Arroyo Hondo Ranch was purchased for $7 million by the Land Trust for Santa Barbara County from rancher J. J. Hollister and co-owners in 2001.

Located 30 miles up-coast from Santa Barbara, between Refugio State Beach and Gaviota State Park, the preserve could very well be the signature property for conservation efforts that encompass the whole Gaviota Coast from Goleta to Point Conception.

The new preserve rises some 3,000 feet in elevation from the Pacific to the upper slopes of the Santa Ynez Mountains in Los Padres National Forest. Hiking opportunities range in difficulty from easy to strenuous in Arroyo Hondo, sometimes termed a "Little Yosemite" for the look of its steep-walled gorge.

Arroyo Hondo is steeped in history. Evidence of a Chumash village, estimated to be 5,000 years old, lies near the creek. Ancient grape vines gone wild twist their tendrils among creekside sycamores. One old trail in the preserve dates to the early 19th century when Chumash and padres used it to travel from the coast to Mission Santa Ynez.

Explore virtually untouched ranch lands . . .

... and a lovely old adobe at Arroyo Hondo.

California history buffs will be intrigued by a visit to the historic adobe, built in 1842 by descendants of José Francisco de Ortega, first commandante of Santa Barbara's Presidio. Later in the century, the adobe served as a stage stop. Longtime ranch manager J.J. Hollister lived in the adobe for ten years until the property's ownership changed hands. The adobe may eventually serve as a museum or visitor center.

The relatively pristine Arroyo Hondo is habitat for the endangered steelhead trout. Other endangered species found in the preserve include the peregrine falcon, tidewater goby and California red-legged frog,

The preserve is managed by The Land Trust for Santa Barbara County, which coordinated fund-raising efforts, including the solicitation of $4 million from the state Coastal Conservancy, as well as other substantial government grants and private donations. Land Trust officials stress that their management philosophy for the preserve will emphasize both careful stewardship and some modest public access. The Trust plans to make only minor improvements to the reserve in the form of improved parking, better trails and some picnic areas.

Arroyo Hondo Preserve is currently open free to the public, by reservation only, on the first and third weekends of the month. Call the Land Trust for Santa Barbara County for more information and reservations: (805) 567-1115.

California Coastal Trail

FOR DECADES, hikers have dreamed of a continuous trail along the beaches and bluffs, and across the mountain ranges of the California coast. This dream is slowly becoming a reality.

When completed, the California Coastal Trail (CCT) will guide ambitious hikers from Mexico to Oregon along a 1,600-mile system of interconnecting beach and coastal range trails. For the less ambitious, the trail will provide days, weekends and weeks of exploration and recreation along one of the most unique environments on earth.

Walk Santa Barbara co-author John McKinney formed the California Coastal Trails Foundation in Santa Barbara in 1983 and scouted a route for the trail. Today's trail, which winds its way from Border Field State Beach on the Mexican border to Pelican State Beach on the Oregon border, passes through a hundred state parks and beaches, plus a few hundred more reserves, county beaches, city beaches, and national parklands.

CCT travels some spectacular coastline in Santa Barbara County, particularly in the county's southernmost shores near Santa Barbara and northernmost coast over the Guadalupe Dunes. While the county has the dubious distinction of having more miles of coastline off-limits to the public than any other coastal county in California, some miles of coastal trail rival the best to be found anywhere in the state.

Gaviota Coast Beaches
California Coastal Trail

*From Refugio State Beach to Tajiguas Beach is 2 miles one way;
to Arroyo Hondo Vista Point is 4.5 miles one way; to San Onofre Beach
is 7.5 miles one way; to Gaviota State Park is 10.5 miles one way*

As the push to secure Gaviota's permanent protection in parkland continues, hikers can sample the recreation potential of this wonderful coastline.

While it may be a few years before Gaviota Coast National Seashore signs are posted on the bluffs, the seashore is currently accessible from several attractive locales in the public domain. Take a drive and a hike and see for yourself what might become the West Coast's second national seashore. (Pt. Reyes is the first such seashore and a useful model for Gaviota.)

Look at the map before you go because Gaviota's geography takes some getting used to. The coast and the Santa Ynez Mountains back of it, extend east-west, which can cause confusion to visitors accustomed to the California coast's usual north-south orientation. In Gaviota-land,

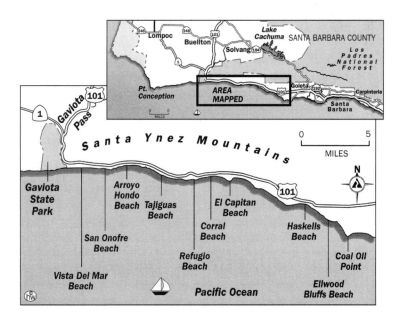

upcoast is west and downcoast is east. Gaviota sunsets are magnificent, even if the sun does seem to set in the north.

A good place to begin an exploration of Gaviota is the 10.5 miles of coast between Refugio State Beach and Gaviota State Park. The two state parklands (vehicle entry fee) have water, picnic areas, plenty of parking, and good beach hiking both up- and downcoast.

Easiest and safest beach-walking is at low tide, particularly in the winter.

Gaviota's coastal trail system does include some bluff trails and coastal access trails, but the best hiking is right on the beach. Hikers enjoy fabulous clear-day views of the four northern Channel Islands—Anacapa, Santa Cruz, Santa Rosa and San Miguel.

Here's a suggested four-stop itinerary for first-time visitors to the Gaviota Coast. For safety's sake, we strongly recommend that you drive upcoast to Gaviota State State Beach, then drive downcoast to access the Gaviota beaches. Legal left turns from westbound Highway 101 are few and far between and not for the faint-hearted motorist. The beaches (small signs, limited parking) are much easier to spot when motoring downcoast.

1. Gaviota State Park: Enjoy the mellow sand strand, walk out on the historic fishing pier for great views. Drive downcoast a few miles to San Onofre Beach.
2. San Onofre Beach: Hike the steep 0.25 mile access trail down the bluffs to this half-mile long sandy beach. Drive downcoast a few more miles to Arroyo Hondo Vista Point.
3. Arroyo Hondo Vista Point: Savor the ocean and island views from the blufftop or from a vintage Coast Highway bridge (closed to vehicles). Trains rumbling across the high trestles over Arroyo Hondo are an impressive sight. Drive 4 more miles downcoast to Refugio State Beach.
4. Refugio State Beach: Hike downcoast one mile to Corral State Beach, a secluded cove, or two miles upcoast to Tajiguas Beach, an even more secluded cove.

Directions: From Highway 101 in Santa Barbara, drive 22 miles upcoast to Refugio State Beach, then 10 more miles to reach Gaviota State Park.

Gaviota Hot Springs, Gaviota Peak
Gaviota Peak Trail

From Highway 101 to Gaviota Hot Springs is 1 mile round trip;
to Gaviota Peak is 6 miles round trip with 2,000-foot elevation gain

Father Juan Crespi of the 1769 Portolá Expedition dubbed the coastline here San Luis, in honor of the King of France. However, the soldiers of the expedition thought that *la gaviota*, Spanish for seagull, was a more apt description.

This walk begins in Gaviota State Park and ends in Los Padres National Forest. You'll visit warm mineral pools, then continue to the top of Gaviota Peak (2,458 feet) for superb views of the Santa Barbara County coastline.

Sometimes this can be a hot hike. During the winter months, however, it can be blustery up on the ridge route. At times the hiker might feel assaulted by clouds, which zoom past, enclosing you in a fog for a few seconds.

Directions: Thirty-five miles upcoast from Santa Barbara, exit Highway 101 at Lompoc/Highway 1 offramp. Turn east a short distance, then follow the highway frontage road 0.25 mile to road's end and the Gaviota State Park lot.

The Hike: Follow the fire road, often strewn with rocks and eroded from winter floods. This is a well-used stretch of trail; most folks walk only to the hot springs and turn back. Leaving behind the highway noise, a half-mile walk beneath spreading oaks and old sycamores brings you to Gaviota Hot Springs.

The springs are more lukewarm than hot. Cross the rock dam, and follow the trail uphill through brush a short distance to a fire road. Bear right.

Ascend the steep fire road, leave behind the oaks and enter a chaparral community. At the top of the ridge, the trail bears right 0.25 mile to Gaviota Peak. On clear days much of the Santa Barbara County coastline, as well as the Channel Islands and Point Conception are visible from the peak.

Gaviota Pass
Beach-to-Backcountry,
Overlook, Hollister Trails

*To Gaviota Pass Overlook is 5 miles round trip with 700-foot elevation
gain; loop via Overlook and Hollister Trails is 8.5 miles round trip
with 800-foot elevation gain*

It would be unfair to say no one stops in Gaviota Pass. The pass hosts a
Caltrans rest area, site of the only public restrooms along a 250-mile
length of Highway 101 between Los Angeles and the hamlet of Bradley
north of San Luis Obispo.

Most motorists who stop, and the multitudes who do not, remain
oblivious to the area's historical importance and natural attractions. Too
bad, because Gaviota Pass and its pathways are too good to pass up.

Most of the pass—the green scene on either side of Highway 101—is
the rolling backcountry of 2,775-acre Gaviota State Park. Park trails
meander across oak-dotted *potreros* and travel ridgetops that afford hikers grand vistas of Gaviota Pass and the wide blue Pacific.

Surely the most memorable view of the pass, to moviegoers anyway,
occurs in *The Graduate* when lost soul Benjamin Braddock (Dustin
Hoffman) drives a beautiful new Alfa Romeo through the mist and into
the Gaviota Tunnel.

Gaviota earned its small place in California history as a place to avoid.
During the short Mexican-American War, General John C. Frémont and
his 700 men were marching south toward Santa Barbara when they
learned that the Spanish *Californio* troops awaited in ambush at Gaviota
Pass. American forces were led through nearby San Marcos Pass by
rancher Benjamin Foxen on Christmas eve 1846. Thus, the Americans
occupied Santa Barbara without bloodshed on Christmas day.

Gaviota State Park offers hiking on both sides of the pass. Eastside
trail attractions include a hot springs and connections to Los Padres
National Forest footpaths.

On the west side of the pass, the park's trail network honeycombs a
delightful backcountry and offers the hiker a number of loops of varying distances and difficulties.

Directions: From Santa Barbara, drive upcoast (west) some 30 miles
on Highway 101. Just as the highway makes a dramatic bend north,
you'll spot a sign for Gaviota State Park. Merge left into the left turn lane
and carefully turn left across the highway onto the state park entry road.

The park road leads to a kiosk (parking fee required) then down to the beach. You'll veer right before the kiosk and follow the unsigned road leading to the exclusive Hollister Ranch community. At the first bend in the road, you'll find the state park trailhead and a pullout for parking on the right.

The Walk: Begin on the asphalt road (closed to vehicles), which leads 0.6 mile across thickets of sweet-smelling sage and fennel on a route parallel to Highway 101. Join the left-forking, signed ("Multi-Use Trail") path as it winds its way to the top of a mustard-splashed hillock. Here you can savor the first of many views of Gaviota Pass.

Next the path climbs more earnestly along a rocky ridge. Intriguing sandstone outcroppings protrude above chamise, ceanothus, manzanita and other members of the chaparral community. Just as your eye is drawn to some (inaccessible) caves across the canyon to your right, the trail deposits you at the mouth of a large cave on your left. The wind-sculpted cave is a large, open-faced recess in the rock where, it's easy to

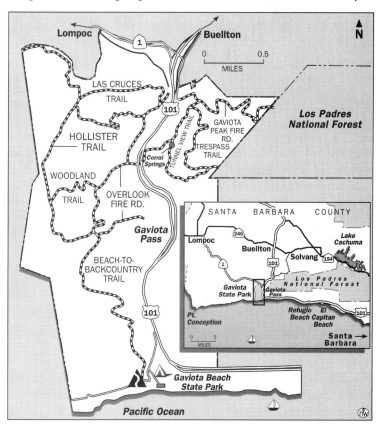

imagine, the native Chumash took shelter or early ranchers waited out the rain.

Beyond the cave, Beach-to-Backcountry Trail dips and rises another 0.5 mile or so before making a final dip to an unsigned junction with Overlook Fire Road. A right on the fire road leads 0.5 mile to a viewpoint occupied only by a radio repeater antenna and a small concrete block building. Turkey vultures roost on nearby sandstone outcroppings, presumably taking in the same view as hikers.

A three-minute walk left on the fire road leads among grand old oaks to another unsigned junction. The fire road bends right (north) while Hollister Trail heads west. I prefer joining Hollister Trail, which ascends west, then bends north along the boundary line between the state park and Hollister Ranch, an exclusive residential community of scattered homes and estates with little or no public access.

Hollister Trail travels a ridgetop and escapes the highway din that can irritate the hiker on other park trails. The trail offers great views over Hollister Ranch and the westward-extending coastline. After about 0.75 mile, the trail passes a junction (often very difficult to spot) with a right-forking connector trail that drops down to meet Overlook Fire Road.

Nearly two miles from its junction with Overlook Fire Road, Hollister Trail reaches a four-way junction. Hollister Trail ascends another 0.25 mile north to a viewpoint, then bends west to the park boundary line.

A right-forking fire road (Las Cruces Trail) descends steeply to a path near, and parallel to, Highway 101; Yucca Trail, signed on the ground but absent from park maps also descends to this path.

Hikers can make a loop trip out of this jaunt by descending on either the trail or the fire road to the footpath near Highway 101. Join an unsigned south-bound trail (overgrown in places) for 0.5 mile to meet Overlook Fire Road and ascend another 0.5 mile to a junction with Beach-to-Backcountry Trail.

Jalama Beach, Point Conception De Anza Trail

From Jalama County Park to just-short of Pt. Conception is 10 miles round trip

At Point Conception, the western-trending shoreline of Southern California turns sharply northward and heralds a number of changes: a colder Pacific, foggier days, cooler air. Ecological differences between the north and south coasts are illustrated by the differing marine life occupying the two sections. Point Conception serves as a line of demarcation between differing species of abalone, crabs and limpets. Climatically, geographically and sociologically, it can be argued that Southern California ends at Point Conception.

This hike takes you along a pristine section of beach and retraces the route of the De Anza Trail, a trail lost to most hikers for more than 200 years. The De Anza Trail was the route of the Juan Bautista de Anza expedition of 1775-76, which brought 240 colonists from Mexico across the Colorado Desert and up the coast to found the city of San Francisco.

On February 26, 1776, the Anza Expedition reached a Chumash village they called *Rancheria Nueva,* just east of Point Conception. Father Font noted the generosity of the Chumash, praised their well-crafted baskets and stone cups, and concluded that the local inhabitants would be good recruits for future missions.

This beach hike leaves from Jalama County Park, the only genuinely public access point anywhere near Point Conception. If the tide is right (be sure to consult a tide table), you can walk to within about a half-mile of the Point.

Public outrage may ultimately see to it that some sort of trail or bike path gives the public access to the coast. In the meantime, be warned that the Bixby Ranch and Hollister Ranch landowners are among the most aggressively anti-coastal-access private property holders in all of California.

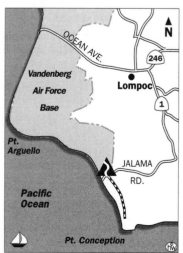

Remember to keep to the beach and don't walk the inland trails onto ranch land.

Directions: Jalama County Park is located 20 miles southwest of Lompoc off Highway 1. From Highway 101, near Gaviota, exit on Highway 1 north and proceed 14 miles to Jalama Road. Turn left and go 14 miles through some beautiful ranch country to the county park.

The Walk: Before heading south over the splendid sand dunes, check the tide table at the park store or at the entry kiosk. As you walk downcoast, you'll soon realize that although Jalama County Park is not on the main Los Angeles-San Francisco thoroughfare, two groups have found it and claimed it as their own—surfers and surf fishermen.

Jalama County Park includes only about 0.5 mile of shoreline, so you soon walk beyond the park boundary. The sandy beach narrows and gives way to rockier shore. Offshore, on the rocky reefs, seals linger. Depending on the tide, you'll encounter a number of sea walls. The smooth tops of the sea walls make a good trail. "1934" is the date imbedded in the concrete walls.

Occasionally, Southern Pacific railroad tracks come into view, though with the crashing of the breakers you can barely hear the passing trains. Since there are no public roads along this section of coast, walking or looking out a train window are the only ways to see this special country. Halfway through your walk, after some lazy bends, the coastline heads almost due south, and the Point Conception Coast Guard Reservation comes into view.

A bit more than 0.5 mile from the lighthouse, you'll run out of beach to walk; passage is blocked by waves crashing against the point. Stay away from the lighthouse and Coast Guard Reservation; visitors are not welcome. A blufftop road and a number of cow trails lead toward the lighthouse, established by the federal government in 1855; however, these routes cross private ranch land and may not be used.

Lompoc
Art Alley Walk

The Santa Barbara County city with the most mispronounced name—it's lom poke, not lom pock—also boasts more nicknames than most. Lompoc is promoted as "The Valley of Flowers," for its prolific commercial flower fields and annual festival celebrating the colorful blooms; "The New Workplace for the New Economy," in recognition of the burgeoning high-tech businesses; "It's a blast," in recognition of the regularly scheduled missile launches from nearby Vandenberg Air Force Base; and "A Friendly Place, with Beauty and Space," paying homage to the affordable housing in pleasant neighborhoods—an important quality of life issue throughout the Central Coast.

Stroll through downtown Lompoc—you might come up with a nickname of your own.

Begin your exploration of Lompoc's magnificent murals by strolling though Art Alley, beginning across the street from the Lompoc Valley Chamber of Commerce, at 111 South I Street (mural brochures are also available at the chamber's office). This unique outdoor art gallery features the work of artists who have interpreted the area's cultural highlights in a variety of ways. The offerings include many history lessons: life of the Chumash people, the Pt. Arguello shipwreck, the Temperance Movement and more.

Continue your discovery of the Lompoc Valley Mural Project throughout the downtown and commercial district. You'll enjoy whimsical flower boxes, floral flags and patriotic themed paintings in every direction.

Don't miss the Lompoc Museum located at 200 South H Street. In 1910, the Carnegie Corporation offered the town of Lompoc a grant to establish a library. The graceful building constructed with those funds today houses the Lompoc Museum. It's a treasure trove of artifacts and information about the Chumash people who once inhabited this area. Pick up a copy of the "Old Town Lompoc Heritage Walk," for a different look at the downtown area.

Ocean Beach
Ocean Beach Trail

From Ocean Beach County Park to Pt. Pedernales is 7 miles round trip

Psssst! Want to know a secret? A military secret? There's a five-mile long beach in the middle of Vandenberg Air Force Base no one knows, where no one goes.

Vandenberg Air Force Base occupies more Southern California coastline than any other private landholder or government agency. The base encompasses some 35 miles of coastline—about the same amount of shore that belongs to Orange County—and public access is severely restricted.

Happily, Santa Barbara County's Ocean Beach County Park puts a small part of Vandenberg's beach within reach. But due to the nesting habits of the threatened snowy plover, parts of this beach are subject to closure at certain times of the year. This wild and windy beach offers a coast walk to remember.

Next to the county park is a large, shallow lagoon at the mouth of the Santa Ynez River. Most of this river's flow is captured high in the Santa Ynez Mountains by a series of dams and Cachuma Lake.

Still, there's enough freshwater, mixed with some Pacific saltwater, to form a 400-acre marsh back of the river mouth. Birdwatchers will especially enjoy spending some time exploring the wetlands. Near the sandbar at the river mouth, birders will spot gulls and sandpipers and perhaps even a nesting colony of the endangered least tern. Patrolling the estuary's cattail-lined tidal channels are mallards, canvas back and ruddy ducks. On the mudflat areas are such migrating shorebirds as willets and long-billed curlews.

After you've visited the estuary, it's time to hit the beach. This walk heads south along windswept Ocean Beach toward Point Arguello. However, before you reach the point, you'll be stopped by another—Point Pedernales—named by the 1769 Portolá expedition when flints, or *pedernales,* were found here. Point Pedernales is about the end of the public beach; besides, the surf crashing against the point is nature's way of telling you to turn around.

Directions: North of Santa Barbara, just past the Gaviota Pass tunnel, exit Highway 101 onto Highway 1 and proceed toward Lompoc. Join Highway 246 heading west toward Vandenberg and drive about 8 miles out of Lompoc to reach signed Ocean Park Road on your right.

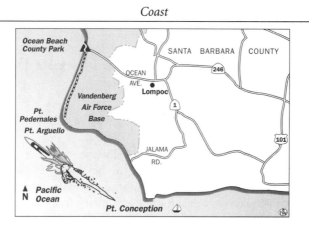

Another sign reads: OCEAN PARK/COASTAL ACCESS. Turn right onto
Ocean Park Road and drive a mile (don't be discouraged by the ugly
approach) past some railroad sidings and freight cars to Ocean Beach
County Park parking lot.

The Walk: Hike over the low dunes, dotted with clumps of European
beach grass, ice plant and hottentot fig, toward the ocean. You'll pass a
couple of pilings sticking out of the sand—the remains of an old fishing
pier. Continue over the sands, sprinkled with sea rocket and sand verbena, to shore. You could walk a mile north on public beach (though
sometimes the Santa Ynez River mouth is difficult to ford), but this day
hike heads south.

After a mile of walking downcoast, the cliffs rise above you and add
to a splendid feeling of isolation. Vandenberg Air Force Base, occupying
the cliffs above, used to be the Army's Camp Cooke until the Army
turned it over to the Air Force in 1957 and it was renamed for Air Force
General Hoyt S. Vandenberg. Atlas ICBMs, Discoverer I, the first polar-
orbited satellite, and missiles of all kinds have been launched from the
base during the last four decades.

Because this stretch of coast bends so far westward, it's ideal for
launches into a polar orbit. Look on the world map and you can see
there's nothing but empty ocean between here and the South Pole; if a
launch fails, the debris will fall on water, not land.

Look for launch pads and towers as you continue downcoast. Ahead
lies dramatic Point Arguello, overlooking the treacherous waters that
have doomed many a ship. One of the worst accidents in U.S. Naval history occurred in 1923 when seven destroyers ran aground just north of
the point.

One of the minor reefs of Point Pedernales will stop your forward
progress. If you have a pair of binoculars, you might be able to spot
some harbor seals sunning themselves on the rocks below the point.

La Purísima Mission State Historic Park El Camino Real Trail

2 to 5 miles or more round trip

Of California's 21 missions, the most fully restored is La Purísima, located four miles north of Lompoc in northwest Santa Barbara County. La Purísima is the only mission with a sizeable amount of land preserved around it—and the only one with hiking trails.

Wandering the thousand acres of hill and dale preserved in the state park will help you grasp that apart from the mission's religious purpose, it was a large commercial enterprise as well—early 19th-century agribusiness. Walk where crops were grown and cattle grazed, view the mission's far-flung waterworks system, and even see the ruts that are reminders of where the old El Camino Real passed through the mission compound.

Following secularization of the mission system, La Purísima was abandoned in 1834 and soon fell into ruin. In 1934, exactly 100 years after the padres left, the Civilian Conservation Corps began reconstructing the church and a whole complex of buildings. Other restoration projects continued intermittently ever since, and today La Purísima is the most completely restored of California's 21 missions.

In addition to the church, tour the soldiers' barracks and the priests' quarters, as well as reconstructions of the granary, bakery, olive press and soap factory. Pens and corrals hold Mexican sheep and cattle, similar to the breeds of the mission period.

At the mission entrance is a small museum, which displays historical information and artifacts recovered from the mission ruins. Enjoy the picnic ground located in a shady grove near the museum.

Twelve miles of park trail explore three different ecosystems. Los Berros Creek flows north-south through Purisima Canyon. West of Purisima Canyon is a large oak-dotted mesa that rises a hundred feet above the canyon floor. East of Purisima Canyon are the stream-cut Purisima Hills.

Local joggers and exercise walkers stick to the park's flatlands by joining El Camino Real, then rounding the barley fields and returning via Las Zanjas Trail. That's a circuit of about 3 miles.

Hikers often use the narrower footpaths—Huerta Mateo and Mesa Arenosa Trails—and make a 2-mile loop. Add the 2-mile loop and the 3-mile together for a fine 5-mile walk in the park.

Directions: From Highway 101 in Buellton, exit on Highway 246 and head west 13.5 miles to Purisima Road. Turn right and proceed a mile to La Purísima Mission State Historical Park on your right. Limited free parking is available near the trailhead alongside Purisima Road or inside the park closer to the mission buildings (fee).

The Walk: From Purisima Road, join La Rancheria Trail to the park museum, walk toward the picnic area, then join paved El Camino Real to signed Huerta Mateo Trail. This footpath leads over sandy terrain. Thriving in the sandy soil is coastal scrub vegetation that normally grows only on dune systems much closer to the coast. Occupying the slopes and ridge crests nearby is a flourishing oak woodland.

Stick with Huerta Mateo Trail past several signed junctions until you reach Cucillo de Tierra, a fire road. Turn left and walk a short quarter-mile to signed Mesa Arenosa Trail. Down you go along this sandy trail until you reach a signed junction with Las Canerias Trail; join this path heading west 0.25 mile to wide Cucillo de Tierra Trail. You can turn right here and head back to the mission buildings; however, those hikers wishing to see more the backcountry will turn left (north) and walk 0.4 mile to El Chaparral Trail, which provides a short connecting route to El Camino Real. Turn left and walk along the flat bottomland of Purisima Canyon, which has been cultivated since the construction of the mission and today supports an annual crop of wheat and barley.

El Camino Real runs out at the park boundary and you turn right (east) on Last Zanjas Trail. This path offers a lovely walk near Los Berros Creek. You'll pass a pond and portions of the old mission aqueduct as you enjoy the 1.25 mile walk back to the mission compound and the trailhead.

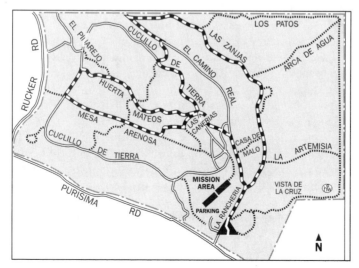

Pt. Sal State Beach

WHEN YOUR EYE travels down a map of the Central California coast, you pause on old and familiar friends—the state beaches at San Simeon, Morro Bay, and Pismo Beach. Usually overlooked is another state beach—remote Point Sal, a nub of land north of Vandenberg Air Force Base and south of the Guadalupe Dunes.

Windy Point Sal is a wall of bluffs rising 50 to 100 feet above the rocky shore. The water is crystal-clear, and the blufftops provide a fine spot from which to watch the boisterous seals and sea lions.

Brown Road/Point Sal Road has a long history of closure, sometimes prompted by rain and sometimes by the Air Force during its missile launches. A few years ago, winter rains washed out the road and the county has chosen not to repair it. Thus, at this writing, travelers have no road access to Pt. Sal.

Point Sal was named by explorer Vancouver in 1792 for Hermenegildo Sal, at that time commandante of San Francisco. The state purchased the land in the 1940s. There are no facilities whatsoever at the beach, so remember, if you pack it in, pack it out.

If you do manage to get to Pt. Sal State Beach, you can walk the beach as well as the bluffs above rocky reefs. Both marine life and land life can be observed from the bluff trail. You'll pass a seal haulout, glimpse tidepools, sight gulls, cormorant and pelicans, and perhaps see deer, bobcat and coyote on the ocean-facing slopes of the Casmalia Hills.

The trail system in the Point Sal area is in rough condition. Families with small children and less experienced trekkers will enjoy beachcombing and tidepool-watching opportunities at Point Sal and the pleasure of discovering this out-of-the-way beach.

Strong hikers can reach Point Sal State Beach by way of a long hike that begins at Rancho Guadalupe County Park. (See Guadalupe Dunes walk, page 148).

When the access road to Point Sal is repaired, here's how to get there: Proceed west past a commercial strip and then out into the sugarbeet fields. Betteravia Road twists north. About eight miles from Highway 101, turn left on Brown Road. Five miles of driving on Brown Road (watch for wandering cows) brings you to a signed junction: leftward is a ranch road, but you bear right on Point Sal Road, partly paved, partly dirt washboard (impassable in wet weather). Follow this road 5 miles to its end at the parking area above Point Sal State Beach.

Santa Maria

2 miles round trip

Located in the verdant Santa Maria Valley, the city of Santa Maria is rightly proud of its designation as an "All-America City" in 1998. Cited for their efforts to make the city a better place to live and work, civic leaders continue the tradition today. With a relatively low cost of living, central location on the California Coast, and a thriving business community, Santa Maria attracts new residents and visitors alike.

A stroll through the downtown area proves Santa Maria offers the amenities everyone has come to expect—more shopping that you can imagine, cultural activities, a colorful history, and even a tradition of excellent barbecue. What could be more American?

Walkers can get a feeling for life at various moments in time in this city, established in 1905, when they take a walking tour of historic buildings and homes. Pick up your copy of *A Walk Through History* at the Santa Maria Valley Historical Society Museum, located next to the Santa Maria Valley Chamber of Commerce at 616 South Broadway, where the walk begins.

Directions: From Highway 101 in Santa Maria, exit on Main Street (Highway 166) and head west to Broadway (135). Turn left (south) and drive 6 blocks to the museum/chamber of commerce buildings and their ample guest parking.

The Walk: The walk takes you north to the mission-style civic center—so graceful that a photograph of the building once appeared in *Life* magazine. The walk continues south on South McClelland Street, an area that is rapidly becoming the heart of the city's cultural district. Home to an eclectic collection of architectural styles and periods, the street boasts the Natural History Museum, located in the oldest house in town; the sparkling, futuristic-looking Abel Maldonado Community Youth Center; and the Discovery Museum, occupying an Art Deco gem that formerly housed a Coca-Cola bottling plant. There is some talk about adding retail shops and restaurants to the area, and even closing it to cars to make it even more pleasant for walkers—we can only hope!

Continue on South McClelland to view the 1928 gem at 801; turn left for a couple of stately homes on East Morrison and then turn right on Speed Street, and right again on East Camino Colegio. Return to Broadway to explore the museum, or to continue the walk, refer to the walk brochure.

Guadalupe Dunes
Guadalupe Dunes Trail

From Rancho Guadalupe County Park
to Mussel Rock is 5.5 miles round trip

If the Southern California coast "ends" at the Santa Barbara County–San Luis Obispo County line—as many geographers and demographers have determined—the grand finale is something to behold. Bold cliffs, towering sand dunes and isolated beaches combine to offer a tableau—and a coastal trek—to remember.

The Santa Maria River forms the Santa Barbara–San Luis Obispo county line. At the river's mouth is a wetland area where several endangered species reside, including the California least tern and brown pelican. Bald eagles and peregrine falcons have been spotted hunting for prey along the riverbanks.

Three miles south of the river is the highest sand dune on the West Coast, 450-foot tall Mussel Rock. It's not really all sand; most of it's actually a rock formation, though there's an ancient sand dune deposited atop it. It's an impressive landmark.

The Mussel Rock Dunes and Guadalupe Dunes south of the Santa Maria River, along with the Oceano Dunes, Pismo Dunes and Callender Dunes to the north, are known collectively as the Nipomo Dunes, the highest and whitest sand dunes in California. These dunes evolved many thousands of years ago, between ice ages, through deposition by the Santa Maria River, and the sculpting of land and sea. The cliffs of Point Sal act as a sand trap to keep the dunes from straying south.

Conservationists have worked for many years to create a large park that would preserve the so-called Mussel Rock Dunes and dramatic beaches and bluffs of the Pt. Sal area.

The beach walk from Rancho Guadalupe Dunes County Park to Mussel Rock is a fine one for the whole family. The beach route, for all intents and purposes, ends at Mussel Rock; hardy hikers will scamper up Mussel Rock and join a rugged unmaintained trail that contours around it, while the less intrepid, and those parties with children, will likely prefer to head inland over the sand dunes or retrace their steps back along the beach. Safest and easiest access to, or exit from, the dunes is by way of one of the gulches located a few hundred yards north of Mussel Rock.

Directions: From Highway 101 in Santa Maria (some 75 miles upcoast from downtown Santa Barbara), exit on Main Street and head west 9 miles to the small town of Guadalupe and a junction with Highway 1. Continue 5 more miles on Main Street to road's end at a beach parking area for Rancho Guadalupe Dunes County Park.

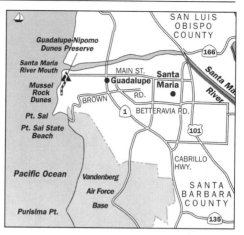

The Walk: Walk south. Tall signposts proclaim the upper (inland) part of the beach as a bird nesting area and informs you to stay away.

In the first mile of your walk, you'll likely encounter the two dominant species of beachgoers in these parts—the surfer trying to catch a big wave and the surf fisherman trying to catch a surf perch or halibut.

After a mile, you'll leave most humans behind, and encounter great numbers of shorebirds. Keep an eye out for some intriguing sea shells, particularly sand dollars. A bit more than two miles out, you can look inland for a route up into the dunes.

Experienced hikers can continue right up to the base of Mussel Rock, scamper up the rock about 30 feet, and join a sandy trail that contours around the rock. The trail passes above a narrow cove, looks down on a small, wave-battered rock arch, and continues south.

Eventually (Mussel Rock is a big rock!) you'll emerge above what locals call Paradise Beach, a sand strand that extends from Mussel Rock to Point Sal.

Dune hikers will enjoy the return sojourn through this Sahara-by-the-Sea. The lower, shifting sand dunes are dotted with sea rocket, sand verbena and morning glory, while the more stable inland dunes are bedecked with lupine, mock heather and the endangered soft-leaved paintbrush.

The highest dunes are closest to Mussel Rock. Savor the fine coastal views south to Point Sal and the 35 miles of pristine coast monopolized by Vandenberg Air Force Base. Northern vistas take in the Nipomo Dunes, Pismo Beach and the sweep of San Luis Obispo Bay.

The Dunes Center

THE MAGNIFICENT COMPLEX of dunes spanning 18 miles of California's Central Coast have a new name and a new center. A portion of the dunes is now part of the Guadalupe-Nipomo Dunes National Wildlife Refuge, so designated to conserve and protect endangered species and habitats.

The Dunes Center, a conservation organization dedicated to preserving the great sandscape, scientific research and visitor education, has an excellent interpretive facility.

Located downtown in the drowsy farming hamlet of Guadalupe, the center is well worth a stop before continuing to the dunes for a hike. Kids will enjoy the hands-on interactive computer exhibits that offer an entertaining and educational tour of the dunes and its denizens, a unique gathering of birds, amphibians and reptiles.

Other exhibits give insights into the colorful history of the dunes, which have been known by a number of names: Pismo, Callender, Oceano, Guadalupe and Nipomo. The dunes are the burial ground of the massive set constructed for the 1923 epic motion picture *The Ten Commandments* directed by Cecil B. DeMille. Learn details about this milestone film and plans to unearth huge statues of Pharaohs and the rest of what was probably the largest set ever made for a silent film.

The center itself is a piece of local history, a lovingly restored 1910 Craftsman house. Arts and Crafts-era aficionados will appreciate a restoration job well done, the home's handsome interior and period furnishings.

The Dunes Center sponsors an ambitious hike schedule that includes the Oso Flaco Sunset Hike, Cecil B. DeMille Birthday Hike, and many more. Other docent-led interpretive walks focus on botanical and zoological life, birdwatching and dune photography.

Local conservationists are working to secure funds for a trail that would lead from the Dunes Center right to the dunes. Such a path would be a great boost to the center's conservation efforts, hiking program and the all-but-overlooked town of Guadalupe.

Directions: From Highway 101 in Santa Maria, exit on Main Street (Highway 166) and drive 9 miles west to an intersection with Highway 1. Turn right (north) on Highway 1 (Guadalupe Street) and drive a mile to the north end of town and the Dunes Center located on the west side of the street.

For more information: The Dunes Center, 1055 Guadalupe Street, Guadalupe, CA 93434; tel.(805) 343-2455.

Center is open Friday through Sunday from noon until 4:30 P.M.

Oso Flaco Lakes
Oso Flaco Trail

To beach is 2 miles round trip;
to Santa Maria River mouth is 8 miles round trip.

The Guadalupe Dunes are a dynamic ecosystem; they've been building up, shifting in response to prevailing northwest winds, for the last 18,000 years or so. Some dunes continue to be formed today. The active, moving ones are those with little or no vegetation.

Flowers, plants and grasses are vital to the dune ecosystem because they stabilize the drifting sands. Brightening the dunes in springtime are sand verbena, coreopsis, daisies and white-fringed aster.

During the Great Depression of the 1930s, the dunes were home to the "Dunites" a motley collection of writers, hermits, artists, nudists and astrologers who lived in driftwood shacks and published their own magazine called *The Dune Forum.*

Shifting sands buried the Dunite community, as they had earlier buried more elaborate developments. In 1904, Oceano boasted beach

Straight as an arrow, this bridge leads to the shifting Guadalupe Dunes.

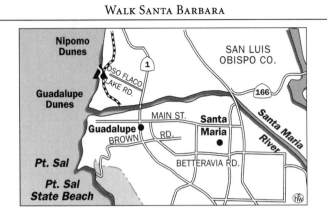

cottages, a wharf, and mammoth La Grande Beach Pavilion. The developer's grandiose plans of turning Oceano into a tourist mecca did not materialize and the pavilion, wharf, and cottages were buried beneath advancing dunes.

This walk passes between Oso Flaco and Lower Oso Flaco lakes to the dunes, then travels down to the beach.

Directions: From Highway 1, some nine and a half miles south of Oceano and three miles north of State Highway 166, turn west on Oso Flaco Road and follow is 3.5 miles to road's end at the dunes. The State Parks collects a parking fee from a kiosk at the trailhead.

The Walk: Follow the narrow, cottonwood-shaded paved road as it passes between the "big" and "little" Oso Flaco lakes. Rails and grebes nest at water's edge, and sandpipers and a rather raucous duck population winter here.

The Portolá expedition camped at the lake in September 1769. The soldiers killed a bear and feasted on it. Although Father Crespi, diarist and spiritual counselor for the expedition, wanted to call the place "Lake of the Martyrs San Juan de Perucia and San Pedro de Sacro Terrato" the soldiers' more humble name of Oso Flaco, or "lean bear," stuck.

You'll cross a bridge over the placid lake waters, then follow a long wooden boardwalk toward the dunes. The trail tops a dune crest and offers fines coastal views from the bold headland above Avila Beach south to Point Sal.

Walk down the dunes to water's edge and head south. Three miles of beachwalking brings you to the Santa Maria River. Among the many native and migratory waterfowl residing at the river mouth are the California least tern and the California brown pelican. Across the river is Rancho Guadalupe County Park and the highest sand dune on the west coast, 450-foot tall Mussel Rock.

Get a good workout on the Guadalupe Dunes.

Country

MOST OF Santa Barbara County is uninhabited, unsullied. Some 630,000 acres of canyons and mountains are government land, within the boundaries of Los Padres National Forest. Santa Barbara County's park system has also preserved some special places. This is a land of great gorges, sandstone cliffs and wide blue sky.

Behind Santa Barbara are the Santa Ynez Mountains, ranging from 2,000 feet to 4,000 feet high. The mountains extend about fifty miles west from Matilija Canyon near Ojai to Gaviota Canyon.

Some of the very best hiking in Southern California is along trails through the mountain canyons right behind Santa Barbara and Montecito. Along with the coast and the city, the countryside has long been an attractive destination for visitors and residents alike. At the start of the 20th century, the Hot Springs Hotel in Hot Springs Canyon was an internationally famed destination—more exclusive than Baden-Baden and other fine European resorts.

And when visitors weren't taking the healing waters they were tramping through the countryside. Even back then, the Santa Barbara Chamber of Commerce promoted hiking and horseback riding in the local mountains.

At first glance on a summer's day, the Santa Ynez Mountains seem smothered with a formless gray mass of brush. On closer inspection, the range reveals much more charm. Antiquarian oaks and sycamores line the canyons and a host of seasonal creeks wash the hillsides. In spring, the chaparral blooms and adds frosty whites and blues to the gray-green plants. The mountains look particularly inviting after the first winter rains. On upper peaks, rain sometimes turns to snow.

The network of trails generally follow creeks to the top of the range. They start in lush canyon bottoms, zigzag up the hot, dry canyon walls, and follow rock ledges to the crest. Many of the trails intersect Camino Cielo (the sky road), which follows the mountain crest. From the top, enjoy sweeping views of the Pacific and Channel Islands, the city and coastal plain.

From the viewpoints, hikers can decipher the region's confusing orientation; that is to say, the east-west direction of the coastline and the mountain ranges. Even many long-time Californians are amused by looking south to the ocean. By all means, consider taking along a map—the Auto Club's Santa Barbara County map is a good one—to help get oriented.

Back of the Santa Ynez Mountains are several more mountain ranges in what geologists call the Transverse Ranges Geomorphic Province, the government calls Los Padres National Forest, and most locals call the Santa Barbara Backcountry. During the first decades of the last century, the backcountry was called the Santa Barbara Forest Reserve. In later years, acreage was added and subtracted, with the backcountry finally coming under the jurisdiction of Los Padres National Forest in 1938.

An estimated 800 miles of trail range through the mountains and the wilderness beyond. Some of these trails have been in use for more than a century while others—Chumash routes—were in use for many, many centuries. Today, thanks to local hikers, conservation organizations, county, state and federal rangers, Santa Barbara has more miles of easily accessible trail than any other community in Southern California.

Romero Canyon
Romero Canyon Trail

From Bella Vista Road, a 6-mile loop through
Romero Canyon with 1,400-foot elevation gain;
11-mile loop through Romero Canyon with 2,300-foot gain

Romero Canyon is the most easterly of the delightful Santa Ynez Mountain trails back of Santa Barbara. Oaks and sycamores shade a year-round creek and a tranquil path.

One meaning of *romero* in Spanish is "pilgrim" and pilgrims of several levels of hiking ability will enjoy a walk through Romero Canyon. Families with small children will enjoy sauntering along its lower creekside stretches. More serious hikers will utilize fire roads to make a moderately graded loop through the canyon, while hikers in top form will trek all the way to Camino Cielo, which offers sweeping views from the crest of the Santa Ynez Mountains.

Directions to Trailhead: From Highway 101 in Montecito, a few miles downcoast from Santa Barbara, exit on Sheffield Drive. Turn right on Sheffield Drive, which briefly parallels the freeway, then swings sharply left (north) toward the Santa Ynez Mountains. Drive 1.5 miles to East Valley Road. Turn left, proceed 50 yards, then make an almost immediate right on Romero Canyon Road. A half- mile along, veer right at a fork in the road, and continue another mile farther to Bella Vista Road. Turn right and continue 0.25 mile to a red steel gate on the left side of the road. Park in a safe manner alongside Bella Vista Road.

The Hike: Walk around the red gate and head up canyon on the fire road. After 0.25 mile of travel, you'll cross a concrete bridge near Romero Creek. About 0.5 mile from the trailhead, you'll cross the creek again. Just after the creek crossing, join unsigned Romero Canyon Trail on your left. Grasses, sedges, bay laurel and a tangle of vines line the creek.

Ascending moderately to steeply, the trail crosses the creek a couple more times, then climbs briskly via switchbacks to a signed 4-way trail intersection.

LOWER LOOP: Turn right where the trail intersects the dirt road and begin your 4-mile descent. After 2 miles of walking, the road offers views of Montecito estates and the coastline, Anacapa and Santa Cruz Islands. The road intersects Romero Canyon Trail 0.5 mile from the trailhead.

UPPER LOOP: Follow signed Romero Trail, which climbs quite steeply over loose shale slopes to the head of the canyon. The trail crests at the top of the Santa Ynez Mountains, about 3,000 feet in elevation. Coastline views are good but the crest here has been scarred by off-road vehicles. From the crest, the trail descends through a brushy, narrow draw toward Camino Cielo. The trail parallels this dirt road for a short ways, then descends to it. Follow Camino Cielo 0.5 mile west to a water tank and the unsigned fire road leading into Romero Canyon. Follow this fire road, which makes a long loop south, then east, then north before dropping into Romero Canyon at the above-mentioned four-way trail intersection.

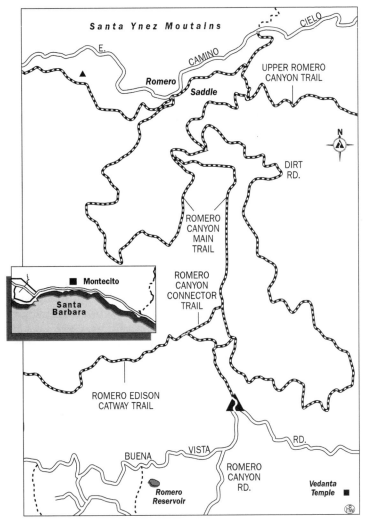

San Ysidro Canyon
San Ysidro Trail

From East Mountain Drive to pools is 3 miles round trip
with 100-foot elevation gain; to East Camino Cielo is 8 miles
round trip with 2,900-foot gain

San Ysidro Trail is attractive and typical of Santa Barbara's foothill trails. It is suitable for several levels of hiking ability. Families with small children will enjoy sauntering along is lower creekside stretches.

A beautiful oak woodland lines San Ysidro Creek. With mighty oaks in the foreground and impressive rock formations in the background, San Ysidro Canyon is a striking scene. Hikers have stacked up rocks to make shallow swimming and wading pools.

The more serious hiker will enjoy sweating up the switchbacks to Camino Cielo. Hungry hikers will enjoy an upscale lunch or dinner at San Ysidro Ranch located very close to the trailhead.

Exploring the wild side of Montecito.

Directions to Trailhead: From Highway 101 in Montecito, take the San Ysidro Road offramp. Drive north on San Ysidro a mile to East Valley Road, turn right and drive a mile to Park Lane, which appears on the left just after crossing San Ysidro Creek. Turn left on Park Lane and in a 0.5 mile veer left onto East Mountain Drive, which passes through a residential neighborhood to the signed trailhead on the right side of the road.

The Hike: The trail, lined with sea fig, bougainvillea, and other exotic plants, parallels a driveway for a short time, passes a couple houses, then becomes a dirt road. Continue up the dirt road and look up occasionally at the handsome Coldwater sandstone formations above you. To your left across the creek is "The Gateway," a popular rock-climbing area. After a half-mile's travel, you'll pass two signed connector trails, which lead to canyons on either side of San Ysidro. To the east is Old Pueblo Trail, to the west Colonel McMenemy Trail.

San Ysidro Trail continues along the bottom of the narrow, snaky canyon. In the springtime, the path may be brightened with blossoms.

Those hikers heading for the upper stretches of San Ysidro Canyon will leave the creek behind and follow the steep rocky trail. Along one length of trail, pipes serve as handrails and you'll feel as though you're walking the precarious Angel's Landing in Zion National Park rather than this supposedly gentle path through the Santa Ynez Mountains. (The rails really aren't necessary.) The trail continues along a rocky ledge, finds more solid ground, then crosses over to the west side of the canyon.

Continue marching through the chaparral up long, steep switchbacks. During the ascent, geology buffs will look up at the Matilija sandstone of the gray-white Coldwater sandstone formation, which has been wind-sculpted into striking cliffs and bluffs. From East Camino Cielo, return the way you came.

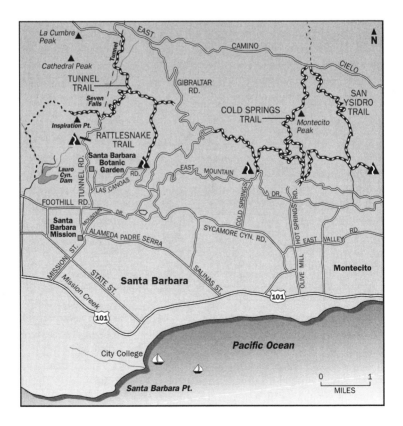

Montecito Connections
San Ysidro, McMenemy, Saddle Rock Trails

From East Mountain Drive to Viewpoint is 2.5 miles round trip
with 500 foot elevation gain; Loop via Girard Trail 3.2 miles
with 1,000 foot gain; Loop via Hot Springs Canyon is 7 miles round trip

For more than a century, hikers have delighted in sauntering the storied canyons in the Santa Ynez Mountains behind Montecito. The creekside paths, the mountain tracks, and the marvelous views of the Pacific, the islands and "America's Riviera" add up to world-class walking.

The only complaint about these canyons that we hikers have made over the years is the lack of connections between canyons. Montecito's trail system has long proved a challenge for hikers who love to loop, who like to ascend one canyon and descend another.

Now, thanks to some new and some improved trail connections, two of Montecito's most attractive canyons—San Ysidro and Hot Springs—can be linked into a memorable jaunt.

The canyon connector trails are useful, but not easy to hike. McMenemy Trail, the lower link between the canyons, is no walk in the park. Because portions of the trail travel within sight of Montecito's magnificent haciendas and it has this close-to-civilization feeling, the hiker is lulled into thinking it's easier going than it is, and surprised by the elevation gained en route.

Edison Catway, the upper link between canyons, is an Edison Company service road bulldozed across the mountains; its purpose is to link the utility's powerline towers. The catway climbs even steeper than Edison's electricity rate hikes.

Between San Ysidro Canyon and Hot Springs Canyon are two north-south connector trails that extend from McMenemy Trail to the Edison Catway. Saddle Rock Trail is an ultra-steep pathway that climbs over and through several prominent rock outcroppings. If "Mountain Goat" is your middle name, you'll love this trail.

An easier, but not easy, north-south way to go, is via the brand new Girard Trail, which climbs from a Montecito overlook to the Edison Catway.

Montecito's trails have long benefited from the watchful eyes of the Montecito Trails Foundation. Founded in 1964 "to expand the trail system in conformity with the county general plan and to preserve old Indian and

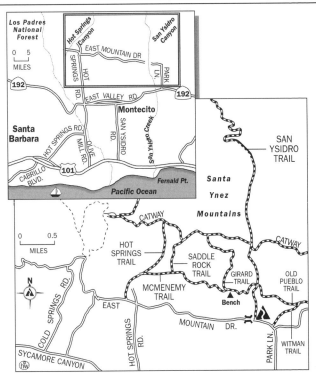

Spanish trails," this volunteer group keeps a watchful eye on some 150 miles of trails that meander from the coast to the summits of the Santa Ynez Mountains in the Montecito, Summerland and Carpinteria communities. The organization is funded mostly by its rather well-heeled membership, supplemented by some small government grants.

MTF provides trail signs, builds new trails and maintains old ones. The organization also helps preserve trail easements and traditional rights of passage that are not always honored by homeowners new to the area or by those expanding their estates. MTF members carefully monitor the local planning process and use both quiet diplomacy and hardball politics to keep trails open to the public.

Directions to Trailhead: From Highway 101 in Montecito, take the San Ysidro Road offramp. Drive north on San Ysidro a mile to East Valley Road, turn right and drive a mile to Park Lane, which appears on the left just after crossing San Ysidro Creek. Turn left on Park Lane and in a 0.5 mile veer left onto East Mountain Drive, which passes through a residential neighborhood to the signed trailhead, located at the back boundary of famed San Ysidro Ranch. Parking is along East Mountain Drive.

The Hike: The trail, lined with exotic plants, winds around the back of a house, then follows a paved road to a wide dirt one. After about 0.5 mile of travel, you'll pass the signed Old Pueblo Trail ascending east, then join the McMenemy Trail leading west.

The path crosses the creek, leads through a eucalyptus woodland, then embarks on a switchbacking ascent across brushy slopes to McMenemy Bench. From the handsome stone bench, enjoy the coastal vistas and ponder your next steps.

My favorite short loop is to join new and unsigned Girard Trail for a steep 0.5 mile ascent to meet the Edison Catway. Then it's a short descent east back to San Ysidro Trail and a mellow return to the trailhead.

For a longer hike, continue west on McMenemy Trail, which soon descends into, and climbs out of, a minor canyon and meets a ridgetop junction with Saddle Rock Trail.

(Saddle Rock Trail climbs very, very steeply to a flat-topped vista point where hikers have painstakingly created a heart from hundreds of small rocks. From "Heart Flat," the path climbs again to the Edison Catway, which leads east to San Ysidro Canyon.)

An easier, more pleasant, but a wee bit longer way to go, is to continue with McMenemy Trail to Hot Springs Canyon. Just before reaching a dirt road (closed to vehicle traffic by a locked gate), take the hiker's bypass trail around the gate and head up the canyon.

The historic road, used to transport guests to a hot springs resort in the horse and buggy days, climbs moderately along the east side of Hot Springs Canyon. Just before this byway crosses San Ysidro Creek, you'll swing right and begin a short climb to ruins of an old resort.

Continue onward and upward on the Edison Catway, which climbs moderately to an unsigned junction with Saddle Peak Trail and to another unsigned junction with Girard Trail, then descends abruptly into San Ysidro Canyon. You'll cross San Ysidro Creek and enjoy the mellow descent through the canyon back to the trailhead.

Hot Springs Canyon
Hot Springs Trail

From Hot Springs Road to the Hot Springs Hotel ruins is 3.5 miles
round trip with 700-foot elevation gain; return via Cold Spring Canyon
is 6 miles round trip with 1,100-foot gain

By the time U.S. soldiers arrived in Santa Barbara in 1847, the "conquest of California" was complete. The war with Mexico was over and at least one Army volunteer, Walter Murray, seemed to have spent most of his enlistment touring the Santa Barbara backcountry and recording his enthusiastic descriptions in a journal.

Particularly impressive to Murray was a pretty canyon aptly named Hot Springs for the sulfurous waters that gushed into bath-size pools.

"The springs would make the fortune of any town in the United States, but here are left alone and deserted, visited only by the native sick or the American sojourner in Santa Barbara," wrote Murray in his *Narrative of a California Volunteer*. "They are remarkably, and very romantically, situated; sequestered from human habitation and almost inaccessible save to the pedestrian."

A decade after Murray's bubbly narrative, Wilbur Curtiss made his way to Santa Barbara—supposedly for health reasons. Curtiss took the cure and left us a story chock-full of clichés: He was suffering from an incurable disease. His doctors gave him but six months to live. Then one day he met a 110-year old native Chumash who attributed his longevity to some secret springs. Curtiss bathed in the springs and experienced a miracle cure. Or so the story goes. . . .

Fable or not, Curtiss soon felt well enough to file a homestead claim on Hot Springs Canyon and begin its commercial development.

In the early 1880s, the homestead became the property of wealthy Montecitans who built a three-story wooden hotel at the springs. Rates were $2 a day, $10 a week, including the baths. Guests enjoyed a library, a billiards room and a well-stocked wine cellar. Another attraction was hiking: Trails meandered around the hillsides and provided excellent panoramas of Santa Barbara and the Channel Islands.

The hotel burned down in 1920, and a small, but still quite posh clubhouse was built on the site. The new spa was even more exclusive: membership was limited to 17 Montecito estate owners who also controlled the Montecito Water Company. Members would telephone the caretaker, tell him to draw a bath, and arrive a short while later by limousine. The club burned down in the 1964 Coyote Fire.

For the next three decades, Hot Springs and its hot pools were accessible to the less affluent. Bathers created rock pools and enjoyed the healing waters. However, hot-spring devotees and the local water company came into conflict over access to the springs. A few years ago the water company sealed off the hot springs with what looks like a World War I bunker. Still, there are hot springs, if you know where to look.

Directions to Trailhead: From Highway 101 in Montecito, exit on Olive Mill Road and head toward the mountains. After intersecting Alston Dive, the road continues as Hot Springs Road. Three miles from 101, you'll reach Mountain Drive. Turn left and proceed 0.25 mile to the signed trailhead on the right side of the road.

MTD: Line 14 Montecito goes up Olive Mill Road to East Valley Road; that's as far as you can get by bus.

The Hike: The trail climbs moderately through a wooded area, skirting some baronial estates. The first few hundred yards of Hot Springs Trail might give you the impression you're on the wrong trail because it crosses and parallels some private driveways. However, keep following the path with the aid of some strategically placed Montecito Trails Foundation signs.

After 0.25 mile of travel, you'll leave the villas behind. The trail veers right, dips into the canyon, crosses Hot Springs Creek and joins a dirt road. The dirt road passes under the embrace of antiquarian oaks, then begins climbing moderately to steeply along the east side of Hot Springs Canyon. Notice the stone culverts and the handsome stone retaining walls as you walk up the old coach road.

A mile's travel along the old road brings you to a junction. A left at the junction puts you on the power-line road that climbs over to Cold Spring Canyon. Stay right, and another 0.25 mile along the road leads to the ruins of the Montecito Hot Springs Club. Stone steps, foundations and exotic flora are about all that's left of the exclusive club.

Return the same way, or follow one of two routes to Cold Spring Canyon. Double-back to the above-mentioned road junction and ascend the power-line road to the ridge separating Hot Springs Canyon from Cold Spring Canyon. Or follow the trail above the resort ruins and climb north, then steeply east over the same ridge.

Once atop the ridge, marred by power-line towers, descend on the unsigned but well-maintained Cold Spring Trail 2 miles through Cold Spring Canyon—which many locals consider the prettiest in the Santa Ynez Mountains. The trail ends at Mountain Drive. Turn left and walk a mile along one of Santa Barbara's more bucolic byways back to your car and the Hot Springs trailhead.

Cold Spring Canyon
Cold Spring Trail

*From Mountain Drive to Montecito Overlook is 4 miles round trip with
900-foot gain; return via Hot Springs Canyon is a 5.5-mile loop; to
Montecito Peak is 7.5 miles round trip with 2,500-foot gain; to Camino
Cielo is 9 miles round trip with 2,700-foot gain.*

Cold Spring Canyon's near-wilderness nature is all the more surprising
when considering its location—scarcely a mile as the orange-crowned
warbler flies from the villas of the rich and famous, and just two miles
from Montecito's boutiques and bistros.

When the Santa Ynez Forest Reserve was established in 1899, rangers
used the trail up the West Fork of Cold Spring Canyon to patrol the
Santa Barbara backcountry. Forest rangers soon realized that this tricky
trail, which climbed around a waterfall and crossed shale slopes, was difficult to maintain. In 1905, the Forest Service built a trail up the East
Fork of Cold Spring Canyon. West Fork lost its status as a government
maintained transportation artery, and the pathway even disappeared
from some maps over the years. (Local hikers, however, never forgot the
wonders of West Fork Trail and today, while little used, it offers a fine
hike. See West Fork Trail description, page 168.)

"Our favorite route to the main ridge was by a way called the Cold
Spring Trail," wrote Stewart Edward White in his 1906 classic, *The
Mountains*. "We used to enjoy taking visitors up it, mainly because you
come on the top suddenly, without warning. Then we collected remarks.
Everybody, even the most stolid, said something."

Cold Spring Trail begins by the alder-shaded, year-round creek, then
rises out of the canyon for fine coastal views. Options abound for the
ambitious hiker and several of them are described below.

Directions to Trailhead: From Highway 101 in Montecito, a few
miles south of Santa Barbara, exit on Hot Springs Road and proceed
toward the foothills for 2.5 miles to Mountain Drive. Turn left. A mile's
travel on Mountain Drive brings you to the Cold Springs trailhead,
which begins at a point where a creek flows over a cement drainage
apron.

The Hike: (See map on page 169) The path rises briefly through oak
woodland, then returns to the creek. On your left, 0.25 mile from the
trailhead, is a junction with West Fork Trail. This century-old trail
ascends 1.5 miles to Gibraltar Road.

Continuing past the West Fork trail junction, the East Fork Trail rises up the canyon wall and rejoins the creek 0.5 mile later. Look for a fine swimming hole below you to the right. The trail then switchbacks moderately out of the canyon to Montecito Overlook. Enjoy the view of the Santa Barbara coastline and the Channel Islands.

If you'd like to loop back to the trailhead via Hot Springs Canyon, you have two options. Easiest way is to take the Edison fire road and make a steep one-mile descent into that canyon. A more challenging route is to ascend Cold Springs Trail another 0.25 mile or so and look for an unsigned connector trail on the right. This path leads down to the ruins of the old Hot Springs Hotel (see Hot Springs Trail description). Once at the bottom of the canyon, you'll descend a fire road to a vehicle gate, then follow a footpath 0.5 mile around and through a residential area down to Mountain Drive. A mile's walk along one of Santa Barbara's more bucolic byways returns you to the Cold Spring trailhead. (While the paths leading into and through Hot Springs Canyon are used by thousands of hikers per year, they are posted "private property.")

From the junction with the Hot Springs connector trail, Cold Springs Trail switchbacks upcanyon and offers fine coastal views. A one-mile climb brings you to two eucalyptus trees (about the only shade en route!) and another 0.75 mile of travel takes you to the unsigned junction with a side trail leading to Montecito Peak (3,214 feet). Enjoy the view!

Cold Springs Trail continues a last mile to Camino Cielo. Many trails lead into the far reaches of the Santa Barbara backcountry.

West Fork, Cold Spring Canyon West Fork Trail

From Mountain Drive to waterfall is 4 miles round trip with 1,000-foot elevation gain

Least known and certainly least traveled of Santa Barbara's foothill trails, the West Fork Trail ventures into some surprisingly wild terrain. Bold sandstone formations, clear springs, lush canyon vegetation and a 200-foot waterfall are few of the considerable charms of this branch of Cold Spring Canyon.

A good time to hike the West Fork is after the first heavy rain of winter. The creek's pools bubble over, innumerable newts take to the trail and the canyon's 200-foot waterfall is a sight to behold.

Geologists contend that West Fork is actually the main fork of Cold Springs Canyon. However, the East Fork has long boasted the main trail, so almost everybody has long regarded the East Fork as the main fork.

As Santa Barbara's foothill canyons go, West Fork is a bit of an odd duck; unlike most other canyons which have a north-south orientation, West Fork extends east-west.

An important note about that waterfall: For most hikers, Cold Spring Canyon's waterfall is a natural wonder to view, not visit. Experienced trekkers can follow a sketchy, soggy creekside route to the base of the falls and even beyond, but this is serious, time-consuming business—slow and often very wet going. Don't underestimate the time needed to complete this journey. Many hikers have been stranded up the creek after dark because they got a lot more hike than they bargained for.

If you have the time for another hike, we suggest the 4-mile round trip hike (with 900-foot elevation gain) up the east fork of Cold Spring Trail to Montecito Overlook.

Directions to Trailhead: From Highway 101 northbound in Montecito, a few miles downcoast from Santa Barbara, exit on Olive Mill Road and drive 2 miles north (toward the mountains) to East Mountain Drive. Turn left and drive a mile to the signed trailhead on the right. Look for the trailhead at a point where Cold Spring Creek flows over a cement drainage apron on Mountain Drive. Parking is along Mountain Drive near the trailhead.

The Hike: The trail immediately crosses the creek to the east side of the canyon. It rises briefly through oak woodland, then returns to the creek. Look to your left, 0.25 mile out, for the signed West Fork Trail. A

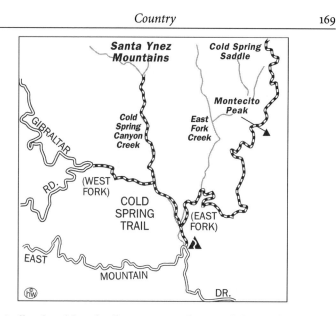

strategically placed bench allows contemplation of the creek bubbling through Cold Spring Canyon.

Cross the creek on West Fork Trail and begin a mellow ascent westward under a canopy of oak and bay laurel. Water pipes, historic and modern, parallel the trail.

After a short mile, look for an unsigned trail on the right leading down to the creek; this is the rough and sketchy path leading north up the canyon to the waterfall.

After this junction, West Fork Trail crosses and re-crosses the creek, then switchbacks in deep shade past ferns, alder and sycamore out of the creekbed onto more open slopes. The trail delivers a view of the waterfall then turns away from it as the canyon narrows and the going gets steeper.

West Fork Trail ends at a hairpin turn of Gibraltar Road, one of the key access roads into the front country of Los Padres National Forest. Until recently, trail's end was a dangerous and noisy unofficial shooting area. The Forest Service has planted a forest of "NO SHOOTING signs along Gibraltar Road and the "plinkers" have apparently packed up their guns and gone elsewhere. These days West Fork Trail's terminus is a much more relaxing place.

Rattlesnake Canyon
Rattlesnake Canyon Trail

*From Skofield Park to Tin Can Meadow is 4.5 miles round trip
with 1,000-foot elevation gain; to Gibraltar Road is 6 miles
round trip with 1,500-foot gain*

Rattlesnake Canyon Trail is serpentine, but otherwise far more inviting than its name suggests.

The joys of the canyon were first promoted by none other than the Santa Barbara Chamber of Commerce. Many early 20th-century visitors to Santa Barbara resorts enjoyed hiking and riding in the local mountains. Eager to keep the customers satisfied, in 1902 the chamber purchased easements from canyon homesteaders to develop a recreation trail.

"Chamber of Commerce Trail," as the chamber called it, was an immediate success with both tourists and locals. However, to the chamber's consternation, both the trail and the canyon itself continued to be called Rattlesnake. Chamber of Commerce Canyon sounded a bit self-serving, so the chamber tried to compromise with an earlier name, Las Canoas Canyon, and adopted a 1902 resolution to that effect.

"The name of Rattlesnake Canyon is unpleasantly suggestive of a reptile," it argued, "which is found no more plentifully there than elsewhere along the mountain range and may deter some nervous persons from visiting that most delightful locality."

In the 1960s, the city of Santa Barbara purchased the canyon as parkland. A handsome wooden sign at the foot of the canyon proudly proclaims: Rattlesnake Canyon Wilderness.

This trail explores Santa Barbara's little wilderness canyon. Red-berried toyon, manzanita with its white urn-shaped flowers, and purple hummingbird sage cloak the slopes and offer a variety of smells and textures. Early in spring, ceanothus blooms and adds frosty whites and blues to the gray-green thickets of chaparral. Shooting stars, larkspur, and lupine also spread their color over the slopes and meadows in spring.

Directions to Trailhead: From Highway 101 in Santa Barbara, go uptown (toward the mountains) on State Street to Los Olivos Street. Turn right and proceed a half mile, passing by the Santa Barbara Mission and joining Mission Canyon Road. Follow this road past its intersection with Foothill Road and make a right on Las Canoas Road. Follow Las Canoas to Skofield Park. Leave your car on the shoulder of the road or in the large parking area near the picnic grounds. The trail begins on Las Canoas Road near the handsome stone bridge that crosses Rattlesnake Creek.

The Hike: (See map on page 160) From the sandstone bridge across from Skofield Park, hike up a brief stretch of trail and join a narrow dirt road that parallels the east side of the creek. For lovely picnicking, take any of the steep side trails down to the creek. In the early 19th century the Mission padres built a dam in the bottom of the canyon, which channeled water into a stone aqueduct and diverted it into

Mr. & Mrs. Lyman Pope at Tin Can Shack, 1916.

the Mission's waterworks system. Portions of the aqueduct still exist and can be seen by the careful observer.

The trail zigzags across the creek, finally continuing along the west bank to open, grassy Tin Can Meadow. The triangular-shaped meadow gets its name from a homesteader's cabin constructed of chaparral framing and kerosene can shingles and sidings. For the first quarter of this century, Tin Can Shack was an important canyon landmark and several guidebooks of that era mention it. It was a popular destination for picnickers who marveled at the inspired architecture and posed for pictures in front of it. In 1925, a brushfire destroyed the shack and it soon disintegrated into a pile of tin.

If you're feeling energetic, hike on toward the apex of the triangular meadow, where you'll find a junction. The trail bearing left leads 0.75 mile and climbs 500 feet to its intersection with the Tunnel Trail—and incidentally to many points of interest in the Santa Barbara backcountry. To the right, Rattlesnake Canyon Trail climbs about 0.75 mile and 500 feet to its intersection with Gibraltar Road. There you will be greeted by an unobstructed view of the South Coast. Watch for strangely patterned triangular aircraft overhead. A favorite hang glider's launch is almost within reach.

Mission Canyon
Tunnel Trail

From Tunnel Road to Seven Falls is 2 miles round trip
with 400-foot elevation gain; to Inspiration Point is 4 miles
round trip with 800-foot gain

Seven Falls has been a popular destination of Santa Barbarans since before the turn of the century. "A pleasant party spent yesterday up Mission Canyon visiting noted Seven Falls and afterward eating a tempting picnic dinner in a romantic spot on the creek's bank," the *Santa Barbara Daily Press* reported in 1887. "To reach these falls requires some active climbing, able-bodied sliding and skillful swinging. . . ."

The seven distinct little falls found in the bed of Mission Creek are still welcoming hikers. This easy family hike in the foothills follows Tunnel Trail, joins Jesusita Trail for an exploration of the Seven Falls along Mission Creek, and ascends Inspiration Point for sweeping coastal views.

Tunnel Trail was used by workers to gain access to a difficult city waterworks project launched by the city of Santa Barbara. Workers burrowed a tunnel through the Santa Ynez Mountains to connect the watershed on the backside of the mountains to the growing little city.

Mission Canyon—from Botanic Garden to backcountry—a delight to explore.

Braving floods, cave-ins and dangerous hydrogen gas, a crew labored eight years and finished the project in 1912.

Mission Creek provided the water supply for Mission Santa Barbara. Near the Mission, which you'll pass as you proceed to Tunnel trailhead, are some stone remains of the padres' waterworks system. Mission Creek also flows through the Santa Barbara Botanic Garden, which is well worth visiting because of its fine displays of native California flora. Paths lead through chaparral, coastal sage and succulent environments to a Mission Creek dam built by the Spanish friars.

A ramble through Mission Canyon, combined with a visit to the Mission and botanic garden, add up to a very pleasant day's outing.

Directions: From Highway 101 in Santa Barbara, exit on Mission Street. Turn east to Laguna Street, then left and drive past the historic Santa Barbara Mission. From the mission, drive up Mission Canyon Road, turning right for a block on Foothill Road, then immediately turning left back onto Mission Canyon Road. At a distinct V-intersection, veer left onto Tunnel Road and drive to its end. Park along the road.

The Hike: (See map on page 160) From the end of Tunnel Road, hike past a locked gate onto a paved road, which eventually turns to dirt as you leave the power lines behind and get increasingly grander views of Santa Barbara. The road makes a sharp left and crosses a bridge over the West Fork of Mission Creek.

Beyond the bridge, you'll hike a short distance under some handsome oaks to a junction. (Tunnel Trail angles northeast, uphill, leading three miles to East Camino Cielo.) You join Jesusita Trail and descend to Mission Creek.

At the canyon bottom, you can hike upcreek into a steep gorge that was cut from solid sandstone. Geologically inclined hikers will recognize fossilized layers of oyster beds from the Oligocene Epoch, deposited some 35 million years ago. In more recent times, say for the last few thousands of winters, rainwater has rushed from the shoulder of La Cumbre Peak and cut away at the sandstone layers, forming several deep pools. If you decide to hike up Mission Creek, be careful; reaching the waterfalls—particularly the higher ones—requires quite a bit of boulder hopping and rock climbing. Even when there's not much water in the creek, it can be tricky going.

From the creek crossing, Jesusita Trail switchbacks steeply up the chaparral-cloaked canyon wall to a power line road atop a knoll. Although Inspiration Point is not all that inspiring, the view from the cluster of sandstone rocks at the 1,750-foot viewpoint is worth the climb. You can see the coastline quite some distance north and south, as well as Catalina and the Channel Islands, Santa Barbara and the Goleta Valley.

Camino Cielo

CAMINO CIELO LEADS to great hiking on the crest of the Santa Ynez Mountains. This lovely mountain road leads to trailheads for Fremont Ridge, Knapp's Castle, La Cumbre Peak, Montecito Peak and more.

Curving east-west across the mid-section of the Santa Ynez Mountains high above Santa Barbara, East Camino Cielo offers the motorist an engaging drive and the hiker access to some top-of-the-world trails.

Camino Cielo is by no means as epic in scale as the Angeles Crest Highway that extends through the San Gabriel Mountains or as celebrated as Mulholland Highway, which twists through the Santa Monica Mountains. And Camino Cielo lacks such "motorist amenities" common to better-known scenic byways such as official vista points, parking, restrooms, and interpretive signs.

What Santa Barbara's very lightly traveled mountain road does offer are views that are second-to-none: to the south is the sparkling coastline and the Channel Islands; to the north are the Santa Ynez Valley, Lake Cachuma and the rugged backcountry of the San Rafael Wilderness.

Figure two hours or so just to take the scenic drive itself. For an introductory loop of about 30 miles, take Highway 101 through Santa Barbara, then up Highway 154 into the Santa Ynez Mountains. Just short of San Marcos Pass, turn on to East Camino Cielo and following it 10 miles along the crest of the range to Gibraltar Road, which brings the traveler back to Santa Barbara. Depending on the number of stops you make and trails you take, an adventure along "the sky road" could extend to a half-day or very full day.

East Camino Cielo is paved, but usually has plenty of potholes. There always seems to be some kind of road repair work in progress. You'll likely spot plenty of warning signs posted about the condition of the road, which is never good, but rarely so bad that it's completely closed to travel.

Fremont Ridge
Fremont Ridge Trail

From East Camino Cielo to Vista Point is 2 miles
round trip with 300-foot elevation gain

Follow in the footsteps of famous pathfinder John C. Frémont on this ridgetop ramble to an overlook of the Santa Ynez Valley. In 1846, Frémont led an American Army battalion south from Monterey. At Christmastime, in extremely heavy rains, the troops struggled over the very muddy Santa Ynez Mountains to "save" Santa Barbara from the Spanish *Californios* and bring it under the America flag.

As another story goes, Chumash workers, under the direction of their missionary overseers, dragged huge pine logs over this ridge. The heavy timbers became the ceiling beams for Mission Santa Barbara, local historians speculate.

This leg-stretcher of a walk, brightened by wildflowers in spring, follows a dirt road down the north slope of the mountains.

Directions to Trailhead: From Highway 154 near the crest of San Marcos Pass, turn east on East Camino Cielo and proceed 1.75 miles to a metal Forest Service gate on the left, as well as parking for a few cars, also on the left side of the road.

The Hike: The first 0.25 mile or so of the ridge route is fairly steep, but it mellows out after that. Views are great from the road, which appears to serve as a fuel break for fire-fighting purposes.

A short mile out, Fremont Ridge begins a drastic decline toward the Santa Ynez Valley. Here's a good point to savor Santa Ynez Valley vistas, take in the panorama of Cachuma Lake and the Los Padres National Forest backcountry and to turn around and return the way you came.

Knapp's Castle

From East Camino Cielo to Knapp's Castle is 1.5 miles
round trip with 200-foot elevation gain

In 1916, George Owen Knapp's recurrent bouts of hay fever sent him high into the Santa Ynez Mountains behind Santa Barbara to seek relief. The wealthy, former chairman of the board of Union Carbide found relief—and an ideal locale to build the mountain home of his dreams.

"This tract, at the edge of the grand canyon of the Santa Ynez Mountains, is one of the most magnificent, in point of scenic glories, in California," reported the *Santa Barbara Morning Press* in 1916.

The high, huge, and presumably hypoallergenic parcel belonged to Homer Snyder, once the chef at Santa Barbara's Arlington Hotel. Back in 1902, Snyder had built a rustic hostelry atop Camino Cielo. Visitors during the early 1900s included Theodore Roosevelt and William Howard Taft. Knapp bought the Snyder place, renamed it Laurel Springs Ranch and charitably offered it as a weekend retreat for Santa Barbara's hardworking nurses and hospital workers.

Knapp's dream home, carved from thick sandstone blocks, took four years to complete. It was a magnificent residence, complete with illuminated waterfalls and a room housing one of Knapp's other passions—a huge pipe organ.

While Knapp was developing his private retreat, he was also helping to boost public access to the Santa Barbara Forest Reserve, as it was known in those days. Knapp and a couple of his wealthy friends were tireless promoters of roads and trails, in order to make the backcountry accessible to all. Knapp's enthusiasm and money helped extend trails west to the top of Refugio Canyon (once part-time rancher Ronald Reagan's spread) and east to Ojai.

The trail-building efforts of Knapp and his buddies were much appreciated by the local populace. As a 1917 editorial in the *Santa Barbara Daily News* put it: "They are strong advocates of the great out-of-doors, and under their leadership places in the wild heretofore denied humans because of utter inaccessibility are being opened up to the hiker and horseback rider."

Knapp was 60-something when he threw himself into his castle-building and trail-building efforts. He spent most of the rest of his long productive life in his castle in the sky. In 1940, he sold his retreat to Frances Holden, who nearly became the first—perhaps the only—

Once a dream house, today Knapp's Castle stands in ruin.

person to lose money in the Santa Barbara real estate market when a forest fire destroyed the castle just five months after she bought it. Fortunately, she had insurance.

Stone walls, part of the foundation, and a couple of chimneys are all that remain of Knapp's Castle. But the view of the Santa Barbara backcountry is still magnificent, particularly if you arrive at sunset and watch the purple shadows skim over the Santa Ynez and San Rafael Mountains.

The upper part of the trail, formerly Knapp's long driveway to his retreat, offers an easy walk down to the ruins from Camino Cielo.

Directions: From Highway 101 in Santa Barbara, exit on Highway 154 and proceed 8 miles to East Camino Cielo. Turn right and drive 2.5 miles to a saddle, where you'll spot a parking area and a locked Forest Service gate.

The Hike: Chamise, ceanothus, toyon and other members of the hardy chaparral family line the old road to the castle. Enjoy fine vistas of the Santa Ynez Valley. After 0.5 mile, the castle comes into view and you continue your descent to the unusual and very photogenic assemblage of walls, arches and chimneys.

From the ruins of Knapp's Castle, enjoy the view of the Santa Ynez River, Cachuma Lake and the wide blue Pacific. And take in the panorama of peaks from Mt. Pinos to Figueroa Mountain to the Casmalia Hills.

La Cumbre Peak

From East Camino Cielo to summit is 0.25 mile round trip
with 100-foot elevation gain

La Cumbre Peak, at 3,985 feet in height, is not the highest summit in the Santa Ynez Mountains but it is a favorite high point for hikers and may just offer the very best views. Panoramas from the peak take in the coast from Pt. Mugu to Pt. Conception, the Channel Islands and the wide blue Pacific. Mountain vistas include the bold backcountry of the San Rafael and Dick Smith wilderness areas.

The Forest Service first constructed a fire lookout atop the peak in the 1920s. The lookout, still standing (barely) today, is of 1945 vintage. The elements and vandals have not been kind to the structure in the years since its abandonment in the early 1980s.

Directions to Trailhead: La Cumbre Peak is accessible from East Camino Cielo, some 9 miles east of its intersection with Highway 154 and 1.8 miles west of its intersection with Gibraltar Road.

The Hike: From East Camino Cielo, simply walk up the asphalt road to the peak. Up top, well-placed picnic tables and benches beckon the visitor to partake of the view. Sandstone outcroppings and stacks of boulders also invite the hiker to sit and enjoy the great vistas.

Adventure Pass

In Los Padres National Forest, an Adventure Pass, which costs $5 a day or $30 a year, is required for parking a vehicle most anywhere within forest boundaries. No pass is needed to access Santa Barbara's foothill trails, but one is necessary to park in other areas of the forest.

An Adventure Pass is required for parking along East Camino Cielo and the Santa Ynez River, on the slopes of Figueroa Mountain and at NIRA Campground.

The monumentally unpopular Adventure Pass (formally named the Recreational Fee Demonstration Program) has proved to be a particularly contentious issue in Los Padres National Forest. If your parked vehicle is ticketed by the Forest Service, you must send a check for $5 to the Department of Agriculture or face a hefty fine.

Recall the words of that great naturalist and tax-resister Henry David Thoreau: "All good things are wild and free," and don't let thoughts of an Adventure Pass intrude on your enjoyment of the backcountry.

Montecito Peak
Cold Spring Trail

From East Camino Cielo to Montecito Peak is 2.5 miles
round trip with 500-foot elevation gain

When viewed from the Santa Barbara side of the range, Montecito Peak is an impressive high point. At 3,214 feet, it's several hundred feet higher than its neighbors. Like lonely sentinels guarding a never-visited outpost, a few isolated eucalyptus trees rise above the chaparral-topped summit, which seems far more than the four miles it actually is from the trailhead.

A shorter and easier (but certainly not easy) way to Montecito Peak is from East Camino Cielo. A mile-long descent leads to the shoulder of the peak, then a wickedly steep and rough 0.25-mile summit trail (best left to experienced hikers) takes you to the top.

Directions to Trailhead: From Santa Barbara, ascend Gibraltar Road 6.5 miles to East Camino Cielo. Turn right and proceed 3.5 miles to a wide turnout, parking and the signed trail all on the right side of the road. From Highway 154, you would travel some 13.5 miles along East Camino Cielo to the start of the trail.

The Hike: The signed path descends from the chaparral-cloaked head of Cold Spring Canyon. After a moderately steep one-mile drop, the path offers views of the Summerland-Carpinteria coastline.

The experienced mountaineer might be tempted to begin bush-whacking up a minor ridgeline to the obvious peak, but it is better to resist this temptation and continue a bit farther down the trail to the unsigned summit trail on the left. A poor trail is better than none, you might acknowledge, as the primitive pathway ascends very steeply up eroded slopes. The trail actually finds firmer footing and gets better as it nears the top of Montecito Peak.

Savor the views of Santa Barbara and sparkling coastline, then be ever so careful when you descend the summit path back to the main Cold Spring Trail.

Aliso Canyon
Aliso Canyon Nature Trail

3-mile loop with 500-foot elevation gain

In a relatively short distance, Aliso Canyon Nature Trail explores a variety of typical backcountry plant communities—oak woodland, grassland and chaparral. The canyon takes its name from white- and gray-barked sycamores (*alisos*) that grow in the canyon.

The loop trail follows Aliso Creek and climbs to a ridgetop viewpoint. Because of its importance, the nature trail earned the federal National Recreation Trail designation.

Even during drought periods when the Santa Ynez River is bone-dry, Aliso Canyon is usually green. The spring wildflower display can include purple lupine, golden California poppies and red Indian paintbrush.

Directions to Trailhead: From Highway 101 in Santa Barbara, take the Lake Cachuma/Highway 154 exit. About 10 miles from Santa Barbara, just over San Marcos Pass, turn right on Paradise Road and drive 4 miles to the signed turnoff on your left for Los Prietos Ranger Station and Sage Hill Campground. (You can pick up a brochure keyed to Aliso Canyon Nature Trail, as well as books and maps, at the ranger station.) Follow the winding road a short distance across the Santa Ynez River and through Sage Hill Campground to the signed trailhead.

The Hike: The trail heads north along the bottom of Aliso Canyon, which is filled with coast live oak and sycamore. You'll soon pass the signed junction with Upper Oso Trail, which comes in from the right; this will be your return route.

After a mile, the path leaves Aliso Canyon, zigzags east up a steep shale slope, then skirts a lovely meadow. Blue-eyed grass, popcorn flower and California poppies dot the meadow, where you'll find a signed junction.

(One trail heads straight ahead [east] to Upper Oso Camp and a junction with Santa Cruz Trail. This trail presents a great opportunity to extend your hike. A mile and a half of travel along Santa Cruz Trail brings you to Nineteen Oaks Camp and four miles of trekking to Little Pine Mountain.)

Aliso Canyon Trail turns right (south) at the junction and switchbacks up the hill to the high point of the nature trail. Enjoy good views of the Santa Ynez Mountains to the south, the San Rafael Mountains to the north.

The flowers that bloom in the spring bring pleasure to all who witness them in Aliso Canyon.

The trail descends sage-covered slopes to the lip of Santa Ynez Canyon, sculpted long ago by the erosive action of the Santa Ynez River. You get a good view of the river, which can be quite a torrent in wet years. On a summer's day during dry years, the river doesn't look like much—just a few shallow pools—but it's actually the longest stretch of free-flowing river in Southern California.

The trail travels along a precipice for a short time, then switchbacks down to the bottom of Aliso Canyon. Near the canyon mouth, you'll intersect the path where you started, head left, and soon return to the trailhead.

homage to Chaparral

On the surface of things, it must be conceded that chaparral lacks the aesthetic appeal of an eastern hardwood forest. California's sun is a thirsty one and for more than half the year, chaparral at close range appears to be a pale brown mass of shriveled herbage.

But look closer at this brown, for it's a very special and beautiful brown, unique to California. The brown of California's backcountry and the brown of the East's backwoods are completely different. Here little snow or rain rots the herbage or drains away its vitality. Chaparral grows ripe and aromatic, bursting with a life that has not been diluted, blanketing slopes and canyons with the effect of bear fur, so that it seems this sun-kissed country has the yielding surface of a living creature. The brown of California is the brown of regeneration; not decay.

One common member of the chaparral community is a stunted version of the oak tree called scrub oak. This squat tree rarely grows taller than man-sized on the southern, of warmer slopes, but often exceeds 10 feet on the northern, or cooler, hillsides. It's one of the most water-conserving members of the community. During the heat of summer, scrub oak leaves discharge a waxy substance, to prevent evaporation. The leaves also curl downward like upside-down spoons to offer less leaf surface to the sun.

To Spanish settlers, scrub oak looked like a plant from back home and that gave it the name *chaparro*. The territory where chaparro grows we now call chaparral, and that is why cowboys wear chaps.

No chaparral inventory would be complete without mentioning wooly blue curls, a bush with elaborate clusters of two-lipped blue-purple flowers covered with a dense purple wool. And Fremontia, ornamenting the brushland with its dark evergreen leaves, yellow flowers and bristly thistles. And aromatic lemonade berry, which guided early California farmers to plant citrus, because where lemonade berry survives the winter, so will lemons and oranges. And California buckwheat, host to a zillion bees. And mountain mahogany, king of the mountain, its short hardwood trunk, leathery leaves and dense profile helping it survive on windswept slopes where nothing else will grow.

Little Pine Mountain
Santa Cruz Trail

From Upper Oso Camp to Nineteen Oaks Camp is 3.5 miles
round trip with 600-foot elevation gain; to Little Pine Saddle
is 10 miles round trip with 3,300-foot gain; to Happy Hollow Camp
is 13 miles round trip with 3,300-foot gain

Santa Cruz Trail presents a lengthy climb, but rewards the hiker with a superb view of the Channel Islands and the Pacific. The trail tops Little Pine Mountain, an ecological island of conifers that one might expect to find only in the High Sierra. Another of this day hike's destinations, ponderosa pine-shaded Happy Hollow Camp, tucked between Little Pine Mountain and a sister peak, is appropriately named.

Hikers can work up quite a sweat while ascending the hot, exposed slope of Little Pine Mountain. Start trekking in the cool of the morning when the trail is shadowed and enjoy your lunch at the top beneath the boughs of a big cone spruce. An ocean breeze usually keeps the mountaintop cool.

Families with young children may enjoy the easy part of Santa Cruz Trail—the first stretch leading to the quiet pools of Oso Creek and to picnicking at Nineteen Oaks Camp. Hikers in good condition or those looking for a good conditioning hike will relish the challenge of the climb to the top of Little Pine Mountain.

Directions to Trailhead: From U.S. 101 in Santa Barbara, exit on California 154 and proceed northwest 11 miles over San Marcos Pass. Turn right onto Paradise Road and follow it east for 6 miles along the Santa Ynez River. Just after crossing the river and passing through a parking area, turn left on Oso Road and follow it a mile to Upper Oso Campground. Hiker parking is provided at the eastern end of the camp at the trailhead.

The Hike: The trek begins at a locked gate beyond the campground and for the first mile follows Camuesa Fire Road. The road stays just to the east of Oso Creek, where there are several fine swimming pools. When the road takes a sharp hair-pin turn, continue straight ahead at a signed junction and join Santa Cruz Trail.

For the next mile the trail is relatively flat, although it drops in and out of washes on the east side of Oso Creek. Soon the hiker sees a signed spur trail on the right, which leads 0.1-mile to Nineteen Oaks Camp. Oaks shade this camp, but not 19 of them. A few tables suggest a picnic.

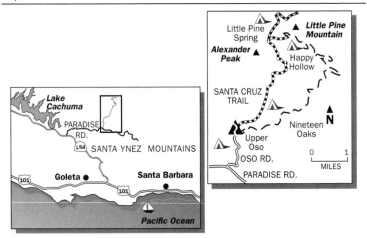

Geologically minded hikers will note the scars in the nearby hills where mercury, also known as cinnabar or quicksilver, was mined.

Santa Cruz Trail heads north, crosses Oso Creek, and begins switch-backing through grassy meadows. Dipping in and out of brush-smoth-ered canyons, you ascend a hill to a saddle between the ridge you're trav-eling and Little Pine Mountain.

The trail soon switchbacks north, then west across the south face of Little Pine Mountain. You'll cross two large mountains, called Mellow Meadows by laid-back Santa Barbarans. The tall dry grass is the habitat of deer and even an occasional mountain lion. The trail climbs around the heads of half a dozen canyons before reaching Alexander Saddle. To the left a bulldozed road goes to 4,107-foot Alexander Peak. Santa Cruz Trail continues straight. You bear right on the connector trail that leads to Happy Hollow Camp.

From Alexander Saddle, the connector trail at first climbs steeply up the dramatic Little Pine Mountain ridgeline. Weather-worn pines on the ridge offer shade and you'll catch fabulous views of the Channel Islands, Santa Ynez Valley, and Lake Cachuma. Large sugar pines and a few live oaks cling to the north face of Little Pine Peak. Farther along the trail you will be among yellow pine, spruce, and Douglas fir. The top of Little Pine Mountain is a great place to unpack your lunch or take a snooze.

From the peak, the trail descends a short way to Happy Hollow Camp, nestled among ponderosa pine, fir, and oak. The camp has a few tables and stoves. During the 1930s, this camp was a recreation site for Civilian Conservation Corps workmen. A handsome field station, re-sembling a châlet, stood here until razed in the mid-1970s. The name Happy Hollow is apt; the camp is indeed in a hollow, and hikers are no doubt happy after the challenging climb.

Santa Ynez River
Santa Ynez River Trail

From Red Rock Trailhead to Gibraltar Dam Picnic Area
is 6 miles round trip with 400-foot elevation gain

Our State Water Resources Control Board suggests that one of the most beneficial uses of the upper Santa Ynez River is for "water contact recreation." Translated from bureaucratic jargon: "Go jump in the river!" Great swimming holes await hikers who venture to the attractive Santa Ynez Recreation Area, located in the mountains behind Santa Barbara.

During dry years, the river's swimming holes are filled by periodic releases from Gibraltar Reservoir, located up-river from the recreation area. Thanks to Santa Barbara's contribution of a small part of its municipal water supply, some of the pools maintain year-round depths of 6 to 18 feet.

Santa Ynez River Trail leads to several pleasant swimming holes and is an easy hike, suitable for the whole family. The most popular ol' swimmin' hole is Red Rock Pool, located only a short distance from the trailhead. The trail to the pools and to Gibraltar Dam Picnic Area follows the remains of an old mining road built in the 1870s during a quicksilver mining boom. The road was later used by workers during the 1920 construction of Gibraltar Dam.

For more information about the Santa Ynez Recreation Area, stop by Los Padres National Forest Los Prietos Ranger Station, located about midway between Highway 154 and Red Rock Trailhead on Paradise Road.

Directions to Trailhead: From Highway 101 in Santa Barbara, take the Lake Cachuma/Highway 154 exit. Proceed east on Highway 154. A short distance over the pass, just past a Vista Point (about 10 miles from Santa Barbara if you're watching your odometer), turn right on Paradise Road and drive to the end of the road—10.7 miles. Leave your car in the large dirt parking lot adjacent to the trail, which begins at a locked gate.

If you're the kind of hiker who loves loop trips, note the presence of a second trail leading from the parking lot to Gibraltar Dam. The "high road," as it's known by locals, makes a gentle traverse across the mountains above the river. Like the "low road"—Santa Ynez River Trail—it's about three miles long. It's a good trail to keep in mind for times of high water.

The Hike: Wide, flat Santa Ynez River Trail passes a NO NUDITY ALLOWED sign and after 0.25 mile crosses the river. Near this crossing you might observe some scattered bricks, all that remain of an early 20th-century quicksilver furnace.

Soon after the first river crossing, you'll reach Red Rock, the most popular swimming hole. Geologically minded hikers will examine the red rock, metamorphosed volcanics of the Jurassic age. Other hikers will plunge into the river.

The trail passes through oak woodland and zigzags from bank to bank along the river. Alongside the river is a canopy of cottonwood, sycamore and willow.

Wildlife-viewing opportunities, particularly during the early morning hours, are quite good near the Santa Ynez River because the area includes several different habitats: oak woodland, coastal sage scrub, grassland and freshwater marsh.

You might spot a deer, gray fox, striped skunk, lizard, cottontail rabbit or raccoon. Watch for pond turtles basking on the rocks, logs and banks of large pools.

The ecological diversity of the area also means a wide variety of birdlife. In the woodland areas, birders might sight a quail, warbling vireo, northern oriole or a woodpecker. Cliff swallows, flycatchers and belted kingfishers swoop over the river.

Several more dry river crossings and a couple of wet ones, and some travel beneath the boughs of handsome coast live oaks, will bring you to Gibraltar Picnic Area, located a few hundred yards down-river from the dam. Oaks shade scattered picnic tables.

You may continue up the trail to Gibraltar Dam, named for the large rock here, which is said to resemble the great guardian rock of the Mediterranean. A second, shadeless picnic site is located at the southeast top edge of the dam. Observe the warning signs at the dam and stay out of restricted areas.

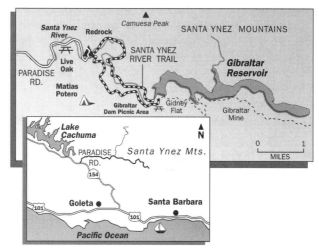

Jameson Reservoir
Old Santa Ynez Fire Road

From Juncal Camp to Jameson Reservoir is 6 miles round trip with 400 foot elevation gain; to Alder Camp is 10 miles round trip with 800-foot gain; to Murietta Divide is 12 miles round trip with 1,600-foot gain

You can't practice your backstroke in it, but it's mighty pretty nevertheless. Jameson Reservoir holds part of Montecito's water supply and is thus off-limits to swimmers, but the oasis-like setting, backdropped by handsome sandstone rocks is attractive to hikers.

The trail is the old Santa Ynez Fire Road, constructed by the Civilian Conservation Corps in the 1930s in order to encourage recreational use of this remote Los Padres National Forest backcountry. Strange as it seems now, this dirt road was once a major route over to Ojai.

The road parallels the upper reaches of the Santa Ynez River and travels to the reservoir and an intersection with Franklin Trail, which leads to Alder Canyon Camp. The camp isn't much, but it has a fairly dependable water supply in Alder Creek.

The trek to Jameson Reservoir and Alder Camp is sufficient for most hikers, but hikers may continue on Santa Ynez Fire Road up to Upper Santa Ynez Camp and then up to Murietta Divide. From the Divide you can descend to Murietta Canyon and Matilija Canyon near Ojai.

Directions to Trailhead: From Gibraltar Road, drive 7 winding miles to Camino Cielo Road. Turn right and follow the road 6 miles to Romero Saddle, then descend 4.6 miles on bumpy dirt road to Juncal Camp on the north bank of the Santa Ynez River. The trail (Santa Ynez Fire Road) begins east of camp at a locked gate.

The Hike: Follow the dirt road along the north side of upper Santa Ynez Valley. En route are oak-dotted meadows. The Santa Ynez River flow varies with the season and releases from the reservoir.

As you approach the reservoir, you'll make a minor ascent, then follow the road along Jameson's edge. A half-mile past the dam, you'll spot a water flume channeling Alder Creek into the river and reach a junction with a road leading right. Join Franklin Trail, crossing a meadow and heading up-canyon along Alder Creek past cascades and pools. The creekside trail, lined with alders, leads a mile to Alder Camp.

From its junction with Franklin Trail, Santa Ynez Fire Road continues along Jameson Reservoir. Above the reservoir is Billiard Flats, a (rather rolling, really) set of meadows.

Past the east end of the reservoir, Santa Ynez Canyon narrows and the fire road begins its two-mile climb to Murietta Divide. All-but abandoned Upper Santa Ynez Camp, another relic from the 1930s, is perched below the divide.

Cachuma Lake
Sweetwater Trail

From Harvey Cove to Vista Point is 5 miles round trip

Cachuma Lake, besides storing an important part of Santa Barbara's water supply, is a popular weekend destination for Southland anglers, campers, birdwatchers and hikers.

Cachuma Lake's trail system is not extensive but does offer boat passengers a chance to get back their land legs and offers a wholly different perspective on the lake and its many species of waterfowl. Those bird watchers who hit the trail will glimpse numerous perching birds in the park's oak woodland—acorn woodpeckers, Western bluebirds, goldfinches, juncos and lots of sparrows.

The lake's Nature Center, headquartered in a 1930s ranch house, has displays about the ecology and history of the Santa Ynez Valley. Exhibits highlight birds, fish, and local flora, as well as the native Chumash who once lived where the lake is today.

The park's best trail is the Sweetwater, which meanders lakeside through an oak woodland to a vista point for a commanding panorama of Cachuma. Oak Canyon Trail, a nature trail, extends 0.75 mile from the Nature Center to the Sweetwater Trail.

Directions to Trailhead: From Highway 101 in Santa Barbara, exit on Highway 154 (San Marcos Pass/Cachuma Lake). Follow the highway

Don't miss the boat; it's the best way to spot waterfowl from near and far.

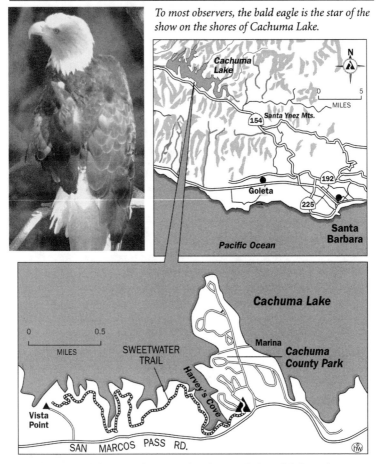

To most observers, the bald eagle is the star of the show on the shores of Cachuma Lake.

20 miles to the lake. Past the entry kiosk, turn left and follow the signs a half mile to Harvey Cove, where you'll find parking for a dozen cars and signed Sweetwater Trail.

The Hike: The first one hundred yards of trail is a paved wheelchair-access route that leads to an oak-shaded picnic area and the Harvey Cove dock. From here, a dirt path follows the far side of the cove for 0.25 mile before angling left into a handsome oak woodland.

A bit more than a mile's hike brings you to Sweetwater Cove, a tiny picnic area perched above the lake. The path joins a dirt road then, as it approaches Highway 154, resumes as a footpath that yo-yos up and down through oak forest before delivering you to Vista Point.

Enjoy the commanding view of Cachuma Lake, bordered on the south by the Santa Ynez Mountains, the north by the San Rafael range, then return the way you came.

Wildlife Cruises of Cachuma Lake

AFTER YOU HIT the trail, board a boat. Cachuma Lake's naturalist-led cruises explore the lake's waterfowl and wildlife. Many visitors like to join the wildlife adventure in winter when migrating bald eagles take up temporary residence at Cachuma.

For birdwatchers planning to travel long distances for the chance to sight a bald eagle, it's almost birdwatching blasphemy to opine that eagles, majestic as they are, often are not the most intriguing part of the boat tour.

Visitors are delighted by the great multitude of birds—the flocks of geese taking flight or the clouds of canvasbacks traveling in long, V-shaped formations.

Sometimes its the antics of the diving ducks that are most remembered. The canvasback, a diving duck with a white back, rusty-red head and long black bill, is almost always sighted on the lake. And visitors are all but certain to see the bufflehead, one of the smallest diving ducks, a chubby white fellow with a black back that buzzes more like a fly than a bird.

Other divers include the small, brown, pie-billed grebe and its cousin, the eared grebe, Because grebes ride stern up in the water, they always seem to be in danger of sinking.

The lake's longest-legged resident is the great blue heron. Its long neck, regal bearing and great size make it one of the most photogenic of birds, and its habit of standing motionless for long periods on one leg make it an easy target for amateur photographers.

Cachuma is not just for the birds. Bobcat, fox and coyote prowl the shoreline. Beaver families live by the lake. Unlike their river-dwelling cousins, Cachuma's beavers don't build dams. Instead, they occupy burrows in the mud banks.

From November through February, the tours focus on migratory birds—in particular the bald eagles that make the shores of Cachuma their winter home. Eagle Tours stay at least 200 feet from the eagles, so photographers should bring fast film, long lenses and perhaps a small tripod. Dress warmly and bring binoculars.

We wholeheartedly recommend the Cachuma Lake wildlife cruises, which depart Fridays, Saturdays, and Sundays. During "Eagle Season," the boat tours are conducted on Wednesday and Thursday as well as the weekends.

For Wildlife Cruise reservations, call (805) 688-4515.

Los Olivos

0.5 mile round trip loop through town

Enjoy a step back in time in lovely Los Olivos, where horse country meets wine country to artful affect. The rustic, yet sophisticated town is filled with galleries, unique shops, restaurants, wine tasting rooms and historical sites that commemorate the ranch life of the Santa Ynez Valley.

Begin your exploration of Los Olivos near the corner of Highway 154 and Grand Avenue ("Main Street" of Los Olivos). Stroll south on Grand to an intersection marked by—one might even say dominated by—a flagpole. After you've explored Grand's two blocks' worth of attractions, relax in tiny Los Olivos Park, walk west on Alamo Pintado Avenue, where you'll note the public library housed in the former Valley Grange building. Don't miss the fanciful garden shop, J. Woeste Treasures, with its whimsical tree house out front, and its treasures beyond the gates.

Turn right on Nojoqui Avenue and look for the Wildling Art Museum on the left. The museum celebrates "America's Wilderness in Art," and is dedicated to promoting a greater understanding of America's wildlands through education, and the collection, preservation and exhibition of art.

Walk past a tall water tower to Mattei's Tavern, built in 1886 to serve travelers who arrived here by stagecoach and railway. Stop for a moment and enjoy the classic wicker-filled sun porch or the warm wood dining room. Continue along Railway Avenue, parallel to the highway back to Grand Avenue, where you began this walk.

Wine-tasting rooms are among the attractions of scenic, historic Los Olivos.

Santa Ynez Valley

WHEN SANTA BARBARANS say they are "going over to the valley" what they are going over is the Santa Ynez Mountains and what they are going over to is the Santa Ynez Valley. Along with Santa Barbarans, legions of visitors from across the nation and around the world are going over to the valley these days.

They go to the valley for two reasons: to sample Santa Barbara County's internationally acclaimed wines, and to savor the valley's stunning scenery, a rustic region of ranches and vineyards framed by two bold mountain ranges.

We wondered if there might be a third reason for going over to the valley: fine wine-country hiking. We fantasized about walking from winery to winery, stopping at each tasting room along the trail. We pictured ourselves sauntering through vineyards—just like in those captivating photographs of walkers among the grapes of Tuscany and Provence displayed in upscale walking tour company catalogs.

(The reality of Santa Barbara wine-country walking proved to be quite a bit different from our fantasies. More about that in a moment.)

Santa Barbara's winemaking tradition is nearly as old as California itself. Spanish padres planted wine grapes around all of California's missions in the late 18th century. Some of the friars' best vineyards proved to be those in Santa Barbara County at Missions Santa Barbara, Santa Ynez and La Purísima.

While Santa Barbara County has long been known as classic "wine country," exactly where in the county to grow the very best grapes poses quite a challenge to growers. Grapes grown too close to the coast suffer from cool lingering fog; those cultivated too far inland, without sufficient maritime influence, suffer in quality as well.

Grape heaven then is a vineyard location that benefits both from a cooling marine layer and lots of long sunny days.

The Santa Ynez Valley has a very long grape-growing season with a 125- to 140-day duration for grapes to ripen, compared to, say, France's Burgundy region, with a 105-day ripening period, and where autumn rains frequently force the harvest. This long, lingering ripening results in better fruit which, when delivered to one of the valley's skilled winemakers, results in exceptional wine.

Part of the art of viticulture is cultivating the right grape in the right place, valley winemakers are quick to point out to we tasters on tour. For more than three decades, the most successful kinds of grapes have proved to be those used to produce the valley's award-winning Pinot Noirs and Chardonnays.

Recently some winemakers have taken advantage of the valley's microclimates to cultivate other kinds of grapes. Andrew Murray Vineyards decided to try Rhône varietals and planted such tongue-twisting grapes as Syrah, Roussanne, Mourvèdre, Grenache and more on steep hillsides.

"Our winery has done really well with the Rhône varietals and pioneered what's now known as 'the Rhone Zone' along Foxen Canyon Road," Fran Murray of Andrew Murray Vineyards told us.

Winemaker Murray is an active member of the Santa Ynez Women Hikers (which number 140 strong, and we mean strong). "The valley is lovely but there aren't many public footpaths," Murray explained.

In fact, there are no public trails. True, the mountains lining the valley—the Santa Ynez range and the wilderness backcountry of Los Padres National Forest—offer superb hiking, but the valley itself has no parkland or public pathways.

"A lot of members of our hiking group would love to see the Wine Trail become a real trail," Murray added.

Ah, the Wine Trail. Spirits soared when we spotted signs along Foxen Canyon Road that read wine trail. Alas, hopes were crushed like grapes at harvest when we learned this "trail" linking wineries is an asphalt two-lane—restricted to motorists and a few brave bicyclists.

Nevertheless, our exploration along Foxen Canyon Road did uncover two wineries—Firestone and Zaca Mesa—where hikers can walk private reserves—as well as taste them. Use a designated driver, be sure to drink lots of water while wine touring and walking.

Our small sampling of Santa Ynez Valley wine-country trails was delightful, but left us thirsting for more. Sure hope our grape expectations are realized, and that Wine Trail becomes a real trail some day.

For more information: Obtain Santa Barbara County Wineries touring map from Santa Barbara County Vintners' Association, (800) 218-0881 or visit www.sbcountywines.com; Firestone Vineyard, (805) 688-3940; Zaca Mesa Winery, (805) 688-9339.

Firestone Vineyard,
Zaca Mesa Winery
Brooks Trail, Windmill Trail

From Firestone Vineyard to Curtis Winery is 2.4 miles round trip;
Zaca Mesa trails are about 0.25 mile long each

Perched atop a commanding mesa overlooking Zaca Canyon, the valley
and the wilderness beyond, Firestone Vineyard is the oldest (established
in 1972) estate winery in the county. The large (by valley standards) winery produces acclaimed Merlots, Chardonnays and Rieslings.

During the 1990s, winery founder Brooks Firestone represented Santa
Barbara County in the State Assembly for a few terms. Returning to the family business, he set about constructing a trail around the vineyard. The fruit
of his labor was Brooks Trail, a pleasant pathway that connects Firestone
Vineyard with Curtis Winery (also owned by the Firestone family).

The signed path begins by the picnic area, located just below the
Firestone tasting room. Valley vistas are superb from the start of the

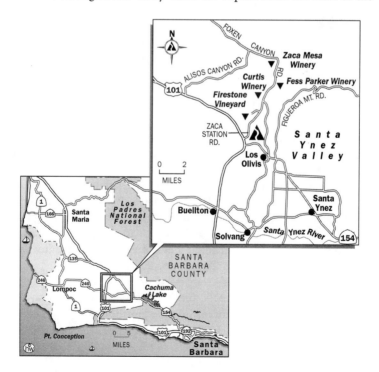

Before its time—wine on the vine. Enjoying the pleasures of Brooks Trail.

trail. The trail descends to the vineyard, skirts rows and rows of grapes, and soon crosses the vineyard's paved entry road.

Brooks Trail climbs a bit, then contours along oak-dotted slopes. Enjoy grand views of Foxen Canyon, then descend to Curtis Winery, which specializes in Rhône-style wines.

Firestone's tasting room is open 10 A.M. to 5 P.M. daily with (rather detailed) winery tours conducted at quarter past the hour until 3:30 P.M. Curtis Winery keeps the same tasting hours as Firestone.

Zaca Mesa Winery (open 10 A.M. to 4 P.M. daily) occupies a serene plateau overlooking Foxen Canyon. Visitors can enjoy an array of Rhône varietals, take two tours (11:30 A.M. and 2:30 P.M.) and take two trails.

Windmill Trail (0.25 mile) climbs to a picnic area then up to a little overlook. Z Trail (0.25 mile) also climbs to an overlook (a popular promontory for exchanging wedding vows). The path winds among the area's two kinds of oak—coastal live and valley—helpfully identified by signs en route.

Directions: From Highway 101, some 45 miles north of Santa Barbara, exit on State Highway 154 (San Marcos Pass Rd.) and head east 2.5 miles to Foxen Canyon Road. Turn left and follow the winding road 4.4 miles to a junction with Zaca Station Road. Firestone Vineyard is located 0.7 mile south on Zaca Station Road. Curtis Winery is just west on the continuation of Foxen Canyon Road.

To reach Zaca Mesa Winery, head north on Foxen Canyon Road.

The most direct route to Firestone Vineyard is to exit Highway 101 on Zaca Station Road and proceed 2.5 miles northeast.

Dojoqui Falls County Park
Dojoqui Falls Trail

To Falls is 0.5 mile round trip

Winter and spring are the seasons to sojourn to Nojoqui Falls, Santa Barbara County's highest and most dramatic waterfalls. A short trail leads through a shady canyon to the seasonal falls, located in a pretty little grotto.

Hidden in an isolated canyon on the north (Santa Ynez Valley) side of the Santa Ynez Mountains near Solvang, Nojoqui Falls County Park is a great rest stop or picnic spot for drives along Highway 101. The park has plenty of picnic sites, as well as softball diamonds and volleyball courts.

Nojoqui, a Chumash word of unknown origin, was once the name of a rancheria under the direction of Mission La Purísima. Now the odd name has been applied to the falls, a canyon, a creek and a county park. The park's wild side features oak woodland and some chaparral-cloaked slopes.

Directions to Trailhead: To reach the park, follow Highway 101 a few miles north of Gaviota Pass, exit on Alisal Road and continue 1.5 miles to the park.

From Solvang, follow Alisal Road 6.5 miles south to the park.

Figueroa Mountain
Davy Brown Trail

From Davy Brown Camp to Harry Roberts Cabin is 3.5 miles
round trip with 900-foot elevation gain; to Figueroa Mt. Rd.
is 6.25 miles round trip with 1,700-foot gain; to Figueroa
Mt. Lookout is 7.5 miles round trip with 2,400-foot gain

Figueroa Mountain, located in Los Padres National Forest 25 air miles behind Santa Barbara, is one of the most botanically intriguing areas in Southern California. The mountain's upper slopes are forested with Coulter pine, yellow pine, and big cone spruce. Spring wildflower displays on the lower slopes are often exceptional. Among the more common roadside and trailside flowers are fiddleneck, Johnny jump-ups, shooting stars, lupine and cream cups.

Tree-lovers will find a variety of arboreal companions, including large specimens of California bay laurel and big leaf maple, and picturesque coastal, valley and blue oaks. At lower elevations are abundant gray pine. Its distinguishing features are long needles in bunches of three and the forking broom-like appearance of its trunk.

On higher slopes grows another three-needled pine: the yellow pine. It's a tall, regal tree with a reddish bark that looks fashioned of rectangular mosaic tiles. And yet another three-needled pine is the Coulter, which produces huge cones, the largest and heaviest of any native conifer.

One good way to explore the mountain's flora and colorful history is to take a hike on Davy Brown Trail, which ascends cool, moist Fir Canyon, climbs to the headwaters of Davy Brown Creek and visits the Forest Service fire lookout atop 4,528-foot Figueroa Mountain. The mountain honors José Figueroa, Mexican governor of California from 1833 to 1835. Anyone who climbs to the mountain's lookout, where there are grand views of the San Rafael Wilderness, Santa Ynez Valley, Point Conception and the Channel Islands, will agree that having such a mountain take your name is indeed an honor.

The trail, as well as a camp and a creek, is named for William S. (Davy) Brown who kept a cabin here during his retirement years, 1880 to 1895. Born in Ireland in 1800, Brown was 80 years old by the time he arrived in the Santa Barbara Backcountry with his two white mules, Jinks and Tommy. If even half of the accounts of his early years are true, he certainly had an adventurous life. He was reportedly an African slave trader, Indian fighter, hunter with Kit Carson, and meat supplier for California '49ers. Though he was considered a recluse, many said that he welcomed visitors into his humble cabin. Davy Brown died in the sleepy Santa Barbara County town of Guadalupe in 1898, having fully experienced the 19th century. His 16-by-20-foot cabin burned in a 1930 fire and is now the site of Davy Brown Camp.

Directions to Trailhead: From Highway 101 in Santa Barbara, exit on Highway 154 and proceed 14 miles over Cachuma Pass and past Lake Cachuma to Armour Ranch Road. Turn right and drive 1.3 miles to Happy Canyon Road. Make a right and wind 14 pleasant miles to Cachuma Saddle Station. To reach the lower Davy Brown trailhead, you'll bear right at the saddle onto Sunset Valley Road and proceed 5 miles to Davy Brown Campground. To reach upper Davy Brown trailhead, bear left at Cachuma Saddle Station onto Figueroa Mountain Road and drive 5 miles to a turnout and signed Davy Brown Trail on your right.

You can also gain access to both trailheads by exiting Highway 101 north of the Buellton turnoff on Highway 154, turning left on Figueroa Mountain Road and driving 15 miles to the upper trailhead. During wildflower season consider a drive up Figueroa Mountain Road and down Happy Canyon Road—or vice-versa—to make a scenic loop through the Santa Barbara Backcountry.

The Hike: From the northwest end of Davy Brown Camp, you'll pass a green gate and a vehicle barrier and join the unsigned trail. You'll head west through forested Munch Canyon, cross Davy Brown Creek a couple of times, then begin angling southwest up Fir Canyon. Actually, no firs grow in Fir Canyon but its southern cousin, the big cone spruce, is plentiful here.

About 1.75 miles from the trailhead, you'll descend into a blue oak-shaded draw and arrive at the ruins of chrome miner Harry Robert's cabin, built in the 1920s. A large big-leaf maple shades the cabin, which is a good lunch stop or turnaround point if you're not feeling too energetic.

Beyond the cabin, maple-shaded Davy Brown Trail crosses and recrosses the creek. Keep a sharp lookout right for the unsigned side trail leading to Figueroa Mountain Lookout. (If you see signed Munch Canyon Spur Trail on your left, you overshot the trail; double back a hundred yards.)

Those wishing to follow Davy Brown Trail to its end will continue ascending along Davy Brown Creek through a wet world of mushrooms and banana slugs under the shade of oaks and laurel. A half-mile from the top of the trail you'll step carefully over a splintered white Monterey shale outcropping at a point where the canyon makes a sharp turn. Old-timers called this bend the Devil's Elbow.

Davy Brown Trail climbs to the headwaters of Davy Brown Creek, then out onto a grassy slope dotted with digger pine and buttercups. You might encounter a herd of bovine forest users on this grassy slope. Trail's end is Figueroa Mountain Road.

Figueroa Mountain Lookout-bound hikers will head right at the above-mentioned junction. The path gains elevation rapidly as it climbs out onto a drier slope cloaked in chaparral—toyon, ceanothus, black sage, scrub oak and mountain mahogany.

The trail descends for a short distance to a tiny meadow then immediately climbs steeply again. As the trail nears the top, notice the progression of pines from digger to Coulter to yellow.

The trail intersects a road to Figueroa Peak. Bear left on the road a half-mile to the lookout. Enjoy the far-reaching views of the major peaks of Los Padres National Forest and of the coast and Channel Islands.

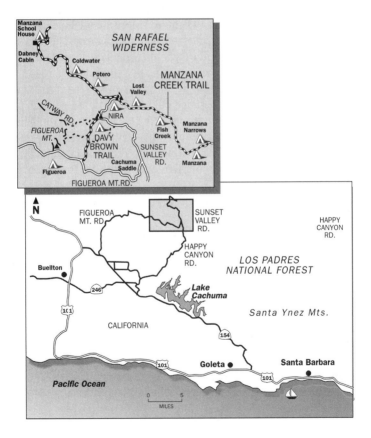

Pino Alto
Pino Alto Trail

0.5 mile round trip

After the September 1993 Murre Fire scorched some of Figueroa Mountain's slopes, the Forest Service got busy making and repairing trails. One new project was Pino Alto (Spanish for "High Pine") Trail, a paved path that's great for outdoor enthusiasts of all abilities, including those in wheelchairs.

Figueroa Mountain's upper slopes are forested with yellow pine, Coulter pine and big cone spruce. The yellow pine is a tall regal tree with a reddish bark that looks fashioned of mosaic tiles. It's a three-needled pine, as is the Coulter, which produces huge cones, the largest and heaviest of our native conifers. Tree-lovers will find plenty of other arboreal companions, including large specimens of California bay laurel and big leaf maple, and picturesque coastal, valley and blue oaks.

The mountain honors José Figueroa, Mexican governor of California from 1833 to 1835. From the mountain's lookout, hikers can enjoy grand views of the San Rafael Wilderness, Santa Ynez Valley, Point Conception and the Channel Islands.

Spring wildflower displays on lower slopes are often good, sometimes exceptional. Among the more common roadside and trailside flowers are fiddleneck, Johnny jumps-ups, shooting stars, lupine and cream cups.

Directions to Trailhead: Getting to Figueroa Mountain can be half the fun. It's a lovely drive through the Santa Ynez Valley into Los Padres National Forest. From Highway 101, about 6 miles north of Solvang, exit on Highway 154 and head five miles to Figueroa Mountain Road in the town of Los Olivos. Turn left and wind 13 miles to the signed turnoff for Pino Alto Picnic Area. Ascend 1.5 miles on a dirt road (suitable for passenger cars) to a handsome picnic area.

For an even more scenic route, leave Highway 101 in Santa Barbara by taking the Highway 154 exit, and traveling 30 miles to Figueroa Mountain Road.

Sedgwick Reserve
Occasional Docent-led walks

Reserve manager Mike Williams describes Sedgwick Reserve as "an untouched piece of old California, what the state looked like 200 years ago."

Wealthy investment banker turned rancher and artist Francis "Duke" Sedgwick recognized both the scientific and aesthetic possibilities of his land. He invited artists out to the ranch and supported their efforts to capture the Old California-style landscape on canvas.

Santa Barbara's Oak Group of painters was particularly effective at evoking the beauty of the land and in raising the public's consciousness about the need to preserve the Sedgwick Ranch. In 1996, Sedgwick Reserve was established; in the opinion of many, it's the jewel in the University of California reserve system.

Perched on the shoulder of Figueroa Mountain, the reserve is an example of what ecologists call extreme topography, that is to say, steep terrain, with creek drainages to match. These sudden changes in altitude and environment add up to an intriguing natural history, one fascinating to scientists and artists alike.

The reserve's most obvious floral feature is its oaks, tens of thousands of them in dense woodlands. (Unfortunately, such oak woodlands are an increasingly rare sight in modern-day California.)

Surely the most photogenic of oaks is the valley oak with its huge canopy, deeply furrowed bark and lobed leaves. Live oaks thrive along creeks while blue oaks (a waxy coating on their non-lobed leaves account for the blue hue) tend to favor hillsides when they're not keeping company with live oaks in woodland gatherings.

Joining the magnificent oaks are several more plant communities, including coastal scrub, chaparral, stands of pine, riparian zones (willows and sycamores along the creeks) and grasslands. Vernal pools are habitat for frogs and toads, as well as rare species of shrimp. More than 300 species of plants have been identified within reserve boundaries.

The reserve is bio-diverse and just plain big. At 5,900 acres, Sedgwick is the largest of the 33 reserves in the University of California system. Scientists say Sedgwick's sheer size enables them to conduct large-scale field experiments on a variety of native ecosystems.

One long-term reserve research project is a study of the reproductive difficulties of the valley oak—a statewide problem. Another important scientific investigation examines how islands of native perennial grasses

It's worth the wait for a guided tour of Sedgwick Ranch.

have managed to survive 200 years of grazing and successfully compete against the introduced grasses that so predominate elsewhere in California.

Because the reserve hosts so many research projects, ranging from studies of bats to global warming, public visitation is, for the most part, restricted to school groups and adult education programs. The Santa Barbara Museum of Natural History and the Santa Barbara Botanic Garden are among the institutions that conduct walks/classes at the reserve. Sedgwick Reserve sometimes hosts "open house" style events with docent-led walks. You'll need a bit of creativity, flexibility and persistence to arrange a visit to the reserve, but such efforts will be well rewarded.

A fine network of old ranch roads and footpaths weaves through the reserve. In the Spring, meadows are brightened by purple lupine, orange poppies and a host of other wildflowers.

Manzana Creek
Manzana Creek Trail

*From NIRA to Lost Valley Camp is 2 miles round trip with
100-foot elevation gain; to Fish Creek Camp is 6 miles round trip
with 400-foot gain; to Manzana Camp is 6.5 miles round trip
with 1,100-foot gain; to Manzana Narrows is
14 miles round trip with 1,200-foot gain*

San Rafael Wilderness was the first Wilderness Area set aside under the federal Wilerness Act of 1964. "San Rafael is rocky, rugged, wooded and lonely," President Lyndon B. Johnson remarked when he signed the San Rafael Wilderness bill on March 21, 1968. "I believe it will enrich the spirit of America."

Manzana Creek Trail begins at NIRA, the major entry point for the San Rafael Wilderness. NIRA, an auto camp and popular day-use area, is an acronym for the National Industrial Recovery Act, a federal program launched during the Depression.

The trail passes tall thin alders and in spring, wildflowers. Four creekside camps beckon the picnicker. In addition to a few stocked trout that survive the legions of fishermen, you'll find frogs, crayfish and turtles in Manzana Creek. Rewarding the hiker after many stream crossings is Manzana Narrows, a narrow part of the canyon where there are some fine pools for fishing and cooling off. Be warned that Manzana Creek can be difficult, even impassable in times of high water.

Directions to Trailhead: From U.S.101 in Santa Barbara, exit on California 154 and follow the latter highway over San Marcos Pass. Beyond Lake Cachuma, turn right on Armour Ranch Road and proceed 2.5 miles to Happy Canyon Road. Make another right and continue 17 miles (Happy Canyon Road becomes Sunset Valley Road after passing an intersection at Figueroa Mountain Road) to NIRA Camp. Parking space for hikers is provided at the south end of the campground.

The Hike: (See map on page 200) Leaving NIRA Camp, the trail immediately crosses Manzana Creek and begins a gentle ascent along the north bank of the creek. The route switchbacks up a low ridge, cloaked with gray pine and soon arrives at Lost Valley Camp, a small site tucked among oak and pine at the mouth of Lost Valley Canyon. This canyon reaches from Manzana Creek up to Hurricane Deck, heart of the San Rafael Wilderness. Lost Valley Trail departs from camp and climbs up to the magnificent deck.

Manzana Creek Trail meanders along the north bank of the creek for the next 2 miles. Look to your right across the creek and you'll spot Fish Creek Camp on the far side of the Manzana flood plain, where Fish Creek meets Manzana Creek. Fishermen like this camp because the creeks here usually support a large trout population.

Past Fish Creek, Manzana Creek Trail at first stays on the north wall of the canyon, passing through chaparral and dipping in and out of washes. Manzana Canyon narrows and the trail angles down toward the creek, which is lined by tall thin alders. The trail crosses the Manzana, and 0.5 mile later, crosses again. The canyon narrows even more and, after a few more creek crossings, the path brings you to Manzana Camp. Located beneath picturesque live oak, the camp offers a dependable water supply, fishing and swimming pools. The manzanita, which gave its name to half the geographical features around here, abounds.Beyond this camp, the trail switchbacks up onto the east wall of the canyon, then soon descends to Manzana Narrows Camp. Wedged in the narrow canyon, the oak- and willow-shaded camp offers pools for fishing and cooling off.

Santa Barbara Calendar of Events

In Santa Barbara, the challenge isn't finding something to do; it's choosing from a dazzling array of activities. We've offered a sampling of some of the more popular annual events.

For a full accounting of any given week's activities, consult the pages of the *Santa Barbara Independent,* the arts and entertainment (free) newspaper. It's distributed every Thursday and always contains interesting articles, reviews of books, restaurants, galleries, movies, plays and architecture, as well as complete listings of all the goings-on in the county.

The *Santa Barbara News-Press* is the city's daily newspaper, the longest continuously published paper in California. Friday editions include "Scene Magazine," with news and reviews about local entertainment, artists and events.

For more information about annual events and seasonal attractions, call the Santa Barbara Conference and Visitors Bureau at 805-966-9222 or visit www.santabarbaraca.com

Annual Events

■ **January**

Whale Watching (through March): boat tours in the Santa Barbara Channel for a look at migrating California gray whales.

■ March

Santa Barbara International Film Festival: enjoy the best in modern cinema with screenings of U.S. and foreign films, tributes to movie stars and the standing room only lectures by Hollywood's most successful screenwriters.

Santa Barbara International Orchid Show: a blooming horticultural happening.

Santa Barbara Kite Festival: Fly high on blustery March winds at beautiful Shoreline Park.

Santa Barbara Whale Festival: celebrate cetaceans of all shapes and sizes.

■ April

Santa Barbara Arts Festival: two weeks of art exhibitions, music, theatre and dance.

Lompoc Spring Arts Festival: enjoy antique vehicles, great entertainment, inspired art and add a little spice with a sanctioned chili cookoff.

Santa Barbara County Vintner's Festival: enjoy the fruit of the vine in nearby Santa Ynez Valley.

Santa Barbara Jewish Festival: discover and take part in the best of Jewish arts, culture, heritage and food.

Earth Day Celebration: festivities at the courthouse, learn how to help the environment.

■ May

Santa Barbara Cinco de Mayo Festival: mariachi music, folk dancing, food and fun.

I Madonnari Italian Street Painting Festival: chalk paintings on the pavement in front of Santa Barbara's Old Mission.

■ June

Big Dog Parade, Santa Barbara: the city goes to the dogs

Santa Barbara County Fair: arts and crafts and old-fashioned fun at the fair.

Santa Barbara Summer Solstice Parade: party every minute of the longest day of the year with whimsical costumes, music and dance, a post-parade gathering at Alameda Park, an evening event at the Sunken Gardens.

Semana Nautica: Summer festival of sports—on land and in the water.

■ July

Santa Barbara French Festival: Francophiles revel in two days devoted to the far-reaching culture of France. Enjoy everything from French bread to a French poodle parade.

Independence Day Parade and Concert: show your patriotic spirit at the parade in the morning, then head over to the Sunken Garden at the County Courthouse for the Santa Barbara Symphony's musical salute to America. Finish the day with fireworks at East Beach.

Santa Barbara Greek Festival: Be Greek for a weekend with food, music and dancing.

■ **August**

Old Spanish Days (Fiesta): Five-day festival celebrating Santa Barbara's heritage. Parades, dancing, concerts, costume parties and more authentic food that you can imagine!

■ **October**

Festa Italiana: Celebrate Santa Barbara's Italian heritage with food, music and fun.

Gay Pride Festival: Santa Barbara celebrates the unity, diversity and individuality of all people

California Avocado Festival: Holy guacamole! Carpinteria serves up an awesome assemblage of avocado appetizers and more.

Goleta Lemon Festival: it's a sweet weekend dedicated to the lovely lemon; music, entertainment and every lemon concoction under the sun.

■ **December**

Christmas Parade: celebrate the holidays with local bands, floats and a special appearance by you-know-who...

Yuletide Boat Parade: Local sailors decorate their watercraft for holiday fun.

Take a Vacation From Your Car

Take the train to Santa Barbara. Use the superb MTD network of bus routes. Ride in a bike cab along State Street or the electric shuttle along the waterfront. Catch a boat to the Channel Islands.

Walk Santa Barbara authors Cheri Rae and John McKinney enthusiastically endorse "Take a Vacation From Your Car," a program that encourages car-free transportation to, and around, Santa Barbara County. Sponsored by the Santa Barbara County Air Pollution Control District, the American Lung Association of Santa Barbara and Ventura counties, plus many other sponsors, the initiative aims to encourage visitors and residents alike to avail themselves of alternative transportation options.

Various hotels and transportation providers offer special incentives and discounts in support of the promotion of Santa Barbara Car Free (and carefree!) programs. Learn more about the Take a Vacation From Your Car project from www.santabarbaracarfree.org

Santa Barbara Metropolitan Transit District
(805) 683-3702
www.sbmtd.gov

Santa Barbara Conference and Visitors Bureau
(805) 966-9222
www.santabarbaraca.com

Resources

City

Ellings Park 805-569-5611
Friends of Franceschi Park
805-564-5418
Goleta Valley Chamber of Commerce
805-967-4618
Lake Los Carneros 805-681-5650
Lotusland Foundation 805-969-9990
Mission Santa Barbara 805-682-4713
Old Town Merchants Association
805-966-4002
Santa Barbara Botanic Garden
805-682-4726
Santa Barbara Cemetery
805-969-3231
Santa Barbara Chamber of
Commerce (Tourist information)
805-965-3021
Santa Barbara Chamber of
Commerce 805-965-3023
Santa Barbara Conference and
Visitors Center 805-966-9222
Santa Barbara Historical Museum
805-966-1601
Santa Barbara Metropolitan Transit
District 805-683-3702
Santa Barbara Museum of Art
805-963-4364
Santa Barbara Museum of Natural
History 805-682-4711
Santa Barbara Shores County Park
805-681-5650
Solvang Visitors and Conference
Bureau 800-468-6765
Trolley Tours 805-965-0353

Coast

Arroyo Burro Beach County Park
805-687-3714
Arroyo Hondo Preserve 805-567-1115
Cachuma Lake Recreation Area &
Campground 805-688-4568
Carpinteria State Beach 805-688-4658
Douglas Family Preserve
805-564-5418
Dunes Center 805-343-2455
El Capitan Canyon 805-968-1033
El Capitan State Beach 805-968-1033
Gaviota Coast Conservancy
805-563-7976
Gaviota State Park 805-968-1033
Jalama Beach County Park &
Campground 805-568-2461
La Purisima Mission State Park
Historic Park 805-733-3713
Lompoc Chamber of Commerce
805-736-4567
Ocean Beach County Park
805-934-6123
Rancho Guadalupe County Park
805-934-6123
Refugio State Beach 805-968-1033
Rincon Beach County Park
805-681-5650
Santa Maria Chamber of Commerce
800-331-3779

Country

Los Padres National Forest
Headquarters 805-968-6640
Mission Santa Ines 805-688-4815
Nojoqui Falls County Park
805-934-6123
Santa Ynez Valley Firestone Vineyard
805-688-3940

Action Friends Sailing Adventures

Enjoy custom sailing charters and instruction out of the beautiful Santa Barbara Harbor on the classic 40-ft. Valiant sailboat, *Grebe.* Take an afternoon or sunset cruise along the coast, or head out to the Channel Islands for couple of days. The mingling of warm and cold currents in the Santa Barbara Channel creates a uniquely rich biodiversity. Dolphins, whales, pinnipeds, and various seabirds are usually encountered. Prices vary depending on activity and number of participants. Call Capt. Hélène Webb for details: (805) 965-8132.

Architectural Foundation of Santa Barbara Walking Tours

Historic Downtown Walking Tours: 1½ hours, docent-led tour; 10 a.m. Saturdays, meet in De la Guerra Plaza; 10 a.m. Sundays, meet at Public Library fountain.

New Domingo Historic Walking Tours: 2-hour docent-led tour cover post-1925 earthquake architecture and history of Santa Barbara; 10 a.m. Sundays, meet at Santa Barbara Public Library, 40 E. Anapamu Street.

Cost is $5 per person. For more information, call the Architectural Foundation of Santa Barbara: (805) 965-6307.

Walk Santa Barbara with The Wayfarers

The Wayfarers, an upscale walking vacation company, hosts week-long walks in such beautiful locales as the New Zealand, Tuscany, Provence and—Santa Barbara! The company features inspired itineraries, graceful lodging, outstanding regional cuisine and expert local leaders.

The Wayfarers' "Santa Barbara, America's Riviera" walk explores the city, coast and mountains. In the enchanting foothills, guests encounter oak woodlands, waterfalls and wildflowers, then ramble miles of picture-postcard beaches. In the Santa Ynez Valley, walkers visit award-winning wineries; Wayfarers walk private reserves—as well as taste them!

Dining experiences embrace the best of California cuisine with a distinctive Santa Barbara twist that includes both Mediterranean and south-of-the-border influences. Local specialties highlight the bounty of the sea and are complemented by fine wines from Santa Ynez Valley vineyards.

The Wayfarers' Santa Barbara Walk is usually led by *Walk Santa Barbara* co-author John McKinney. To learn more about the company's deluxe walking vacations, call 1-800-249-4620 or visit them on the web at: www.thewayfarers.com

Index

About the Authors

Cheri Rae The award-winning editor of national magazines, from *Bicycle Sport* to *Runner's World,* has written extensively about Santa Barbara's cuisine, culture and children's activities. Her books include *Sunrooms, Mojave National Preserve: A Visitor's Guide* and that regional favorite, *The Santa Barbara Bargain Book.* She served as the style editor of *Santa Barbara Magazine* and is a contributing editor to the *Santa Barbara Independent.* Cheri lives in Santa Barbara with her co-author husband, John, and two children.

John McKinney The long-time *Los Angeles Times* hiking columnist is the author of a dozen walking and nature guides including *Day Hiker's Guide to Southern California,* one of the best-selling trail guides of all time. John writes articles and commentaries about walking for national publications, promotes hiking and conservation on radio and TV, and serves as a consultant to the walking tour and hiking products industries.

For more information about *Walk Santa Barbara* and walking elsewhere in America and abroad take a hike to

www.thetrailmaster.com